NARRATOLOGY AND BIBLICAL NARRATIVES:

A Practical Guide

D. F. Tolmie

NARRATOLOGY AND BIBLICAL NARRATIVES:
A Practical Guide

D. F. Tolmie

WIPF & STOCK · Eugene, Oregon

Wipf and Stock Publishers
199 W 8th Ave, Suite 3
Eugene, OR 97401

Narratology and Biblical Narratives
A Practical Guide
By Tolmie, Francois
Copyright©1999 by Tolmie, Francois
ISBN 13: 978-1-62032-479-0
Publication date 7/31/2012
Previously published by International Scholars Publications, 1999

For Ansa, Carmien, Francois and Mialise

CONTENTS

Abbreviations	ix
Illustrations	xi
Acknowledgments	xiii
Chapter One: Introduction	1
Why Study Narratology?	1
The Basic Framework	5
Chapter Two: Narrator and Narratee	13
Defining the Narrator and the Narratee	13
A Typology of Narrators and Narratees	15
The Functions of a Narrator	21
Chapter Three: Focalization	29
Focalization or Point of View?	29
Procedures for Analyzing Focalization	32
Examples from Biblical Narrative	33
Chapter Four: Character	39
The Process of Characterization	41
Classification of Characters	53

Chapter Five: Events	63
Surface Structure of Events	64
Deep Structure of Events	67
Chapter Six: Time	87
Order	87
Duration	93
Frequency	99
Chapter Seven: Setting	
Analyzing Settings in Biblical Narratives	105
Chapter Eight: Implied Author and Implied Reader	115
The Implied Author in John 13:1-30	117
The Implied Author's Textual Strategy	130
Bibliography	145
Index of Subjects	153
Index of Authors	157
Index of Scripture References	161

ABBREVIATIONS

ABR	Australian Biblical Review
Bib	Biblica
BTB	Biblical Theology Bulletin
CBQ	Catholic Biblical Quarterly
ET	Expository Times
EThL	Ephemerides Theologicae Lovanienses
EvQ	Evangelical Quarterly
HebStud	Hebrew Studies
Interpr	Interpretation
JBL	Journal of Biblical Literature
JETS	Journal of the Evangelical Theological Society
JR	Journal of Religion
JSNT	Journal for the Study of the New Testament
JSOT	Journal for the Study of the Old Testament
JThS	Journal of Theological Studies
LingBib	Linguistica Biblica
Neotest	Neotestamentica
NT	Novum Testamentum
NTS	New Testament Studies
PMLA	Publications of the Modern Language Association of America
PRSt	Perspectives in Religious Studies
RExp	Review and Expositor

RStR	Religious Studies Review
SR	Studies in Religion
StTh	Studia Theologica
ThD	Theology Digest
ThR	Theological Review
ThTo	Theology Today
TS	Theological Studies
YR	Yale Review
ZAW	Zeitschrift für die alttestamentliche Wissenschaft
ZNW	Zeitschrift für die neutestamentliche Wissenschaft

ILLUSTRATIONS

Figure 1: Narratological Framework	6
Figure 2: The Actantial Model	57
Figure 3: Actants in John 13:1-17:26	58
Figure 4: Actants in John 13:1-17:26	59
Figure 5: Semiotic Square	69
Figure 6: Semiotic Square (Genesis 2:4b-3:24)	76
Figure 7: Semiotic Square (Acts 27:1-44)	81
Figure 8: Actants in John 13:1-30	123
Figure 9: Semiotic Square (John 13:1-30)	126

ACKNOWLEDGMENTS

For the last fifteen years I have been privileged to be engaged in the application of narratological models to Biblical literature (in particular New Testament narratives). I hope that this book will serve in some way to introduce other people to this wonderful way of reading the narratives in the Bible. As the subtitle indicates this book is intended as a *practical* introduction, and therefore I have tried to keep to the basic issues that are important when one wants to do a narratological analysis. However, at the end of each chapter the interested reader will find a list of suggestions for further reading referring him/her to relevant works - some of which present a wider scope or even other approaches to narratology.

I wish to express my gratitude to the University of the Orange Free State that provided valuable financial assistance enabling me to visit overseas libraries in order to finish this book.

Earlier versions of Chapters Four and Five appeared in *Acta Theologica* 18/1: 50-76 and *Ekklesiastikos Pharos* 78/1: 76-95 respectively and are included with permission.

Biblical quotations, unless otherwise noted, are from the New Revised Standard Version of the Bible, copyright 1989 by the Division of Christian Education of the National Council of the churches of Christ in the USA. Used by permission. All rights reserved.

Bloemfontein, South Africa
July 23, 1998.

CHAPTER ONE

INTRODUCTION

Why study narratology?

"Narratology" - or "narrative criticism"[1] as it is often called - can be defined as the systematic study of the typical features of narrative texts. Narratology is based on the assumption that certain characteristics (universals) are found in *all* narrative texts - from antiquity until modern times. These characteristics are then integrated and presented in terms of narratological frameworks that can be used for the analysis of individual narrative texts.

The first question to be answered is to what extent narratology can be of help in exegesis. To answer this question it is important to realize that, in terms of length, more than one third of the Hebrew Bible and more than half of the New Testament consist of narratives! If this is recognized, it seems self-evident that the dynamics of narrative should be high on the agenda of Biblical scholars. Strangely enough, it has taken them literally centuries to realize the importance of this facet for exegesis!

For more that two centuries Biblical scholars have been involved in ways of reading narrative texts that have constantly shifted their attention from the narrative dynamics of the text to a reconstruction of the way in which the text developed. For example, this century has seen the flourishing of various methodological frameworks in this regard. *Source criticism* was developed in order to delineate the sources that were used in the composition of the final texts. *Form criticism* was developed in order to analyze and describe the setting within which individual units of tradition functioned before they were incorporated into the texts. *Redaction criticism* was developed with the aim of describing the way in which the authors edited and combined their sources in the process of writing. Needless to say, very valuable research has been done and is still being done along these lines. Nevertheless, in this process an important facet of narrative texts, namely that they are *narrative* texts, did not receive enough attention. However, during the last decade or so attempts have been made to focus attention on the narrative dynamics of texts. This happened in the following way:

In the case of the Hebrew Bible one of the great German Biblical scholars, Herman Gunkel (1862-1932), had already drawn attention to certain aspects of the narrative dynamics of texts. In his commentary on Genesis[2] he discussed the artistic quality of this Bible book, and amongst other things pointed out the way in which the narratives were divided into "scenes", the differences between main and secondary characters, the ways in which persons were characterized in the narratives, the use of dialogue, and the importance of events in the structuring of the narratives - all aspects which are usually considered in a narratological analysis. Unfortunately this aspect of Gunkel's work was not continued in Biblical scholarship. Instead, research focused on the other issues he addressed, namely the analysis of the history of forms and genres in the Hebrew Bible.[3] One notable exception is the book by Erich Auerbach, *Mimesis. The Representation of Reality in Western Literature*,[4] that was published in 1946. Auerbach was not a biblical scholar, but a literary critic, and as the title of his book indicates, he had a much wider interest than merely the Bible. However, his insistence that Biblical narratives could be studied in terms of the procedures used in general literary criticism was a very important contribution. For example, he compared the scene of Odysseus' homecoming in Homer with the scene of God's appearance to Abraham (Gen 22). Although he praised Homer's brilliance as revealed in the way the scene is composed, he, nevertheless, indicated that he preferred the way in which the Bible presents reality. According to him the emotions, psychological complexities and emotional power of Biblical characters are beyond the scope of Homer's characters:

> Far from seeking, like Homer, merely to make us forget our own reality for a few hours, it seeks to overcome our reality: we are to fit our own life into its world, feel ourselves to be elements in its structures of universal history.[5]

Another literary critic that made a major contribution in this regard is Northrop Frye who condemned the underlying assumption in the historical critical approach to the Bible. According to Frye historical critics read the Bible as if it were only a scrapbook of corruptions, redactions, glosses, insertions, misplacings, conflations and misunderstandings. Instead he argued that the underlying assumption should be that the whole Bible has a typological unity, a single archetypal structure, extending from creation to apocalypse.[6] This principle he later worked out systematically in his *The Great Code: The Bible and Literature*.[7] Another important contributor was Meir Sternberg. His *The Poetics of Biblical Narrative. Ideological Literature and the Drama of Reading*[8] was devoted to an analysis of (mostly) the Hebrew Bible as a *literary* work. Sternberg investigated aspects such as the configuration of point of view, temporal structure, the development of the plot and the means of characterization in order to indicate the ideological thrust of the narratives. During the 1980s the number of narrative-critical analyses of the Hebrew Bible or parts of it steadily increased. To mention but two: *Poetics and Interpretation of Biblical Narrative*[9] by Adele Berlin and *Narrative Art in the Bible*[10] by Shimon Bar-Efrat.

In the case of the New Testament the first signs of a new approach began to appear in the 1970s. At first, the development of this approach was almost exclusively limited to the study of the Gospel of Mark - largely due to the influence of the Markan Seminar of the *Society of Biblical Literature*. The new approach that was followed came to be called "narrative criticism" and was based on two propositions that distinguished it from the historical-critical approach to the Gospels: Firstly, an approach based on the assumption of the *wholeness* of the Gospel of Mark replaced the traditional approach that was based on the assumption that it was a fragmented work. Secondly, Markan scholars placed more and more emphasis on the narrative character of this Gospel. They started acknowledging the fact that it tells a story about Jesus, events, persons and places, and that these aspects could be studied independently of the other aspects that were usually emphasized in the historical-critical approach.[11] Amongst the first studies that were published in this regard were those of Norman Petersen, David Rhoads and Donald Michie. By analyzing story time and plotted time Norman R. Petersen[12] proved (against the conclusions of eminent scholars such as Wilhelm Wrede, Karl Ludwig Schmidt and Rudolf Bultmann) that the Gospel of Mark is a *plotted* narrative. He also discussed the relationship between the narrated and the real world in Luke-Acts. David Rhoads and Donald Michie[13] presented the first detailed analysis of the Gospel of Mark in terms of aspects such as the function of the narrator, settings, plot and character. Soon the method of narrative criticism was also applied to the Gospels of Matthew, Luke and John.[14]

From this short overview it is clear that in recent years there has been a major shift with regard to the way in which Biblical texts are interpreted. Exciting new avenues for research have been opened! The aim of this book is to introduce you to the field of narratology in such a way that you will be able to see the usefulness of this approach for exegesis without being burdened by an overwhelming amount of technical detail. Accordingly I shall only discuss basic issues and present but one of quite a number of frameworks that can be utilized in the exegesis of narrative texts. At the end of each chapter you will find suggestions for further reading that will enable you to find books and articles that will give you much more detailed information with regard to the issues discussed.

The basic framework

The theoretical framework that I discuss in this book is based on the work of narrative critics such as Gérard Genette,[15] Shlomith Rimmon-Kenan,[16] Mieke Bal[17] and Seymour Chatman.[18] These persons are all well-known narratologists in the field of theory of literature and have all developed detailed theoretical frameworks for the analysis of narrative texts. These frameworks are based on insights derived from major developments in theory of literature during this century, such as Anglo-American New Criticism, Russian Formalism, French Structuralism, Phenomenology of Reading, and Reader-Response Criticism.[19]

As a starting point a basic framework is needed. Since the process whereby a narrative is transmitted from the author to the reader must basically be viewed as a process of communication, it seems best to use a model developed for analyzing communication as the basic framework. Of the various communication models available I have chosen a model developed by Seymour Chatman[20] and adapted it slightly:

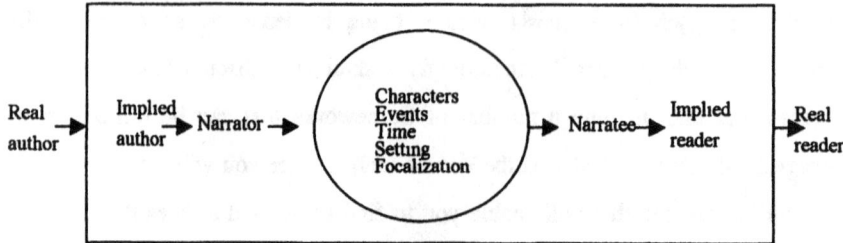

Figure 1

Of the participants in the narrative communication situation identified in the diagram above the concepts "real author" and "real reader" are the easiest to understand. The concept "real author" is used to refer to the person(s) who actually wrote the narrative text. In the case of Biblical narratives one should often think in terms of a plurality of persons in this regard since, in many cases, quite a number of persons were involved in the creation of the text. The concept "real reader" is used to indicate the actual person who is reading the narrative text - in this case, it will be you and I.

The other terms are more difficult to define. I shall discuss the concepts "implied author" and "implied reader" in this chapter. The rest will be discussed in the following chapters.

The concept "implied author" is open to misunderstanding as a result of the different and even contradictory ways in which it is used - not only by Biblical scholars, but also by literary critics. Therefore it is always very important to make sure how it is defined when used by another scholar, as well as to make perfectly clear how you understand it when you use it. Basically the various approaches in this regard can be reduced to two options. The first option is to define the implied author in the sense of "the author as implied by the narrative" or "the idea of the author that is formed in the mind of the reader as s/he reads the narrative text". This is the way in which the term is used by Wayne Booth:[21]

> As he (= the author) writes, he creates not simply an ideal, impersonal "man in general" but an implied version of "himself" that is different from the implied authors we meet in other men's works... However impersonal he may try to be,

> his reader will inevitably construct a picture of the official scribe who writes in this manner - and of course that official scribe will never be neutral toward all values... The "implied author" chooses, consciously or unconsciously, what we read; we infer him as an ideal, literary, created version of the real man; he is the sum of his own choices.

The second option is to use the concept in a depersonified sense. If it is used in this way, it is not defined primarily in terms of its relationship to the real author, but in terms of the narrative text itself. To put it simply, it is defined in terms of the *overall textual arrangement*. Chatman,[22] for example, defines the implied author as the organizing principle in the text, responsible for the total textual arrangement. He also emphasizes that, although the implied author has no direct means of communication (like the narrator), it instructs the reader through the design of the whole text. In this book I shall be using the term "implied author" in this sense.

In order to analyze and discuss the implied author of a narrative text in terms of this option, we shall thus have to analyze the total textual organization of the narrative text including all the aspects indicated in the diagram above: narrator and narratee, characters, events, time, setting and focalization. These aspects will all be discussed in the following chapters. After this has been done, the various aspects must then be integrated in order to outline the overall strategy of the implied author (see chapter 8). It is also very important to realize that, in the case of Biblical narratives, the overall textual strategy of the implied author usually has a very specific ideological thrust (it could also be called a theological thrust) in the sense that this strategy is usually aimed at persuading the implied reader to accept a certain evaluative perspective.

This brings us to the next question, namely what is meant by the concept "implied reader". With regard to this question the confusion amongst critics is even worse than with regard to the definition of the implied author. If one starts reading books and articles in this regard, one soon finds oneself confronted with a bewildering range of descriptions of the reader in/of the text, for example, the ideal reader, the hypothetical reader, the informed reader, the authorial reader, the intended reader, the super-reader, the average reader, the encoded reader and the actual reader![23] Once again, most of these concepts can be reduced to two basic options: On the one hand, the definition of the implied reader can focus very strongly on the real reader in one way or another, usually in the sense of the reader that the real author had in mind when s/he wrote the text[24] or the kind of real reader presupposed by the text. On the other hand, it can be depersonified and instead be linked closely to the text itself. As in the case of the concept "implied author", I shall follow the trend that depersonifies the concept "implied reader" and links it strongly to the text itself.[25] Thus, when I use the concept "implied reader" I shall not be referring in any way to a real reader of flesh and blood, neither to the intended reader in the sense of the reader that the author had in mind when the narrative was written, but I shall understand it as an intratextual literary construct, functioning as a counterpart of the implied author.

Willem Vorster's[26] definition serves as a good summary of what I understand by "implied reader" in this book:

> The reader in the text is a literary construct, an image of a reader which is selected by the text. It is implied by the text, and in this sense it is encoded in the text by way of linguistic, literary, cultural, and other codes. It is not identical to any outside flesh-and-blood reader. It is an image that is created by the author which has to be constructed by the real reader through the reading process in order to attribute meaning to the text, that is to actualize the text. The construction of the reader in the text is central to the establishment of the meaning of a narrative according to this view.

A last question remains to be answered: If the implied author and the implied reader are both defined as intratextual constructs, is there any difference between the two? In this regard I shall follow Jeffrey Staley[27] whose distinction between the two concepts is to my mind the best. He describes the difference between the two concepts in terms of the difference between the *linearity* (implied author) and the *temporality* (implied reader) of the text. According to this distinction the implied author should be seen as the overall textual strategy in the sense of a static overarching view of the narrative text, whereas the implied reader is described in terms of the temporal quality of the text in the sense that the overall textual strategy of the text is revealed word by word, sentence by sentence, paragraph by paragraph, from the first word in the text until the last. The following quotation from Staley[28] provides one with a good description of the difference between implied author and implied reader:

> While the implied author knows the text forward and backward, the implied reader only has knowledge of what has been read up to the given moment. It is thus encoded in the unidirectional, forward movement of the text, and as such, does not know what word comes next in the text, nor does it stop reading until the narrative is ended. Although the implied reader has a perfect knowledge and memory of what has been read, it is nevertheless limited by its temporal status. An implied reader must also gain all its knowledge of the story from the medium itself, even if the general outline of the story is known in a culture...

In the last chapter I shall give a practical illustration of the way in which this distinction can be used.

Suggestions for further reading

Alter, Robert, & Kermode, Frank. *The Literary Guide to the Bible*. Cambridge: Belknap Press, 1987.
Alter, Robert. *The Art of Biblical Narrative*. New York: Basic Books, 1981.
Bar-Efrat, Shimon. *Narrative Art in the Bible*. Sheffield: Almond, 1989.
Beardslee, William A. *Literary Criticism of the New Testament*. Philadelphia: Fortress Press, 1970.
Berlin, Adele. *Poetics and Interpretation of Biblical Narrative*. Sheffield: Almond, 1983.
Clines, David J. A., Gunn, David M., and Hauser, Alan J. Eds. *Art and Meaning. Rhetoric in Biblical Literature*. Sheffield: JSOT Press, 1982.
Eco, Umberto. *The Role of the Reader. Explorations into the Semiotics of the Text*. London: Hutchinson, 1979.
Frye, Northrop. *The Great Code: The Bible and Literature*. New York: Harcourt Brace Jovanovich, 1982.
Gibson, Walker. "Authors, Speakers, Readers and Mock Readers", in *Narratology. An Introduction*, eds. Susana Onega & José Angel García Landa, (London: Longman, 1996), 155-160.
Funk, Robert W. *The Poetics of Biblical Narrative*. Sonoma: Polebridge, 1988.
Iser, Wolfgang. *The Act of Reading: A Theory of Aesthetic Response*. Baltimore: Johns Hopkins University Press, 1978.
Iser, Wolfgang. *The Implied Reader: Patterns of Communication in Prose Fiction from Bunyan to Bennett*. Baltimore: Johns Hopkins University Press, 1978.
Kermode, Frank. *The Genesis of Secrecy: On the Interpretation of Narrative*. Cambridge: Harvard University Press, 1979.

Longman, Tremper. *Literary Approaches to Biblical Interpretation.* Grand Rapids: Zondervan, 1987.
McKnight, Edgar. *The Bible and the Reader. An Introduction to Literary Criticism.* Philadelphia: Fortress, 1985.
Moore, Stephen D. *Literary Criticism and the Gospels. The Theoretical Challenge.* New Haven: Yale University Press, 1989.
Petersen, Norman R. *Literary Criticism for New Testament Critics.* Philadelphia: Fortress, 1978.
Powell, Mark Allan. *What is Narrative Criticism?* Minneapolis: Fortress, 1990.
Staley, Jeffrey L. *The Print's First Kiss: A Rhetorical Investigation of the Implied Reader in the Fourth Gospel.* Atlanta: Scholars Press, 1988.
Sternberg, Meir. *The Poetics of Biblical Narrative. Ideological Literature and the Drama of Reading.* Bloomington: Indiana University Press, 1985.
Van Tilborg, Sjef. "The Gospel of John: communicative processes in a narrative text", *Neotest* 23/1 (1989), 19-31.

Notes

[1] Many exegetes prefer the term "narrative criticism", but I prefer the term "narratology". See Steven Cohan and Linda M. Shires, *Telling Stories. A Theoretical Analysis of Narrative Fiction* (New York: Routledge, 1988), 53:

> Narratology studies narrative as a general category of texts which can be classified according to *poetics*, the set of identifiable conventions that make a given text recognizable as a narrated story. Narrative poetics outlines the competence required of readers and tellers of narrative. Like language (*langue*), narrative can be understood as a system underlying individual texts: narrative poetics is to given narrative what grammar is to a given utterance, so a reader's knowledge of how narrative operates as a system partly determines the sense he or she makes of a text. Such competence is not limited to so-called literary texts or even to fictional ones. It is, moreover, culturally learned, reinforced by narratives of all sorts: novels, short stories, and films, of course, but also newspapers, advertisements, histories, myths, letters, anecdotes, jokes, popular entertainment, and public ceremonies.

See also Gérard Genette, *Narrative Discourse.* Translated from the French by Jane E. Lewin (Oxford: Basil Blackwell, 1980), 22.

[2] See Herman Gunkel, *Genesis* (Göttingen: Vandenhoeck & Ruprecht, 1977, First published 1901), xxvii-lvi.

[3] See Shimon Bar-Erat, *Narrative Art in the Bible* (Sheffield: Almond, 1989), 9-10.

[4] Original title: *Mimesis. Dargestellte Wirklichkeit in der abendländischen Literatur* (Bern: Francke, 1946). English translation by Willard Trask (Garden City: Doubleday, 1957).

[5] Ibid., 12.

[6] Northrop Frye, *Anatomy of Criticism. Four Essays* (Princeton: Princeton University Press, 1957), 315.

[7] Northrop Frye, *The Great Code: The Bible and Literature* (New York: Harcourt Brace Jovanovich, 1982).

[8] Bloomington: Indiana University Press, 1985.

[9] Sheffield: Almond, 1983.

[10] Sheffield: Almond, 1989.

[11] Stephen D. Moore, *Literary Criticism and the Gospels. The Theoretical Challenge* (New

Haven: Yale University Press, 1989), 7-8.

[12] Norman R. Petersen, *Literary Criticism for New Testament Critics* (Philadelphia: Fortress, 1978).

[13] *Mark as Story. An Introduction to the Narrative of a Gospel* (Philadelphia: Fortress, 1982).

[14] Examples of such studies are the works of Werner H. Kelber, *Mark's Story of Jesus* (Philadelphia: Fortress, 1979); O. C. Edwards, *Luke's Story of Jesus* (Philadelphia: Fortress, 1981); Charles H. Talbert, *Reading Luke: A Literary-Theological Commentary on the Third Gospel* (New York: Crossroad, 1982); Richard A. Edwards, *Matthew's Story of Jesus* (Philadelphia: Fortress, 1985); Jack Dean Kingsbury, *Matthew as Story* (Philadelphia: Fortress, 1988), *Conflict in Mark. Jesus, Authorities and Disciples* (Minneapolis: Fortress, 1989) and *Conflict in Luke: Jesus, Authorities, Disciples* (Minneapolis: Fortress, 1991).

[15] *Narrative Discourse* (Oxford: Basil Blackwell, 1980).

[16] *Narrative Fiction: Contemporary Poetics* (London: Metheuen, 1983).

[17] *Narratology: Introduction to the Theory of Narrative*. Translated from the Dutch by C. van Boheemen (Toronto: University of Toronto Press, 1985).

[18] *Story and Discourse: Narrative Structure in Fiction and Film* (Ithaca: Cornell University Press, 1978).

[19] See Mark Allan Powell, *What is Narrative Criticism?* (Minneapolis: Fortress, 1990), 11-23, in this regard.

[20] *Story and Discourse*, 147.

[21] See Wayne C. Booth, *The Rhetoric of Fiction* (Chicago: Chicago University Press, 1961/1983), 71-75.

[22] *Story and Discourse*, 148. See also Willem S. Vorster, "The Reader in the Text: Narrative Material", *Semeia* 48 (1989): 23-24, and Jeffrey Staley, *The Print's First Kiss: A Rhetorical Investigation of the Implied Reader in the Fourth Gospel* (Atlanta: Scholars Press, 1988), 27-30. How important it is to distinguish clearly between real author, implied author and narrator, can be seen in Sjef van Tilborg's discussion of these issues in John's Gospel in his *Imaginative Love in John* (Leiden: E J Brill, 1993), in particular pp. 96-100 and 103-110.

[23] Robert M. Fowler, "Who is the 'Reader' of Mark's Gospel?" in *SBL Seminar Papers 1983*, ed. Kent Harold Richards, (Chico: Scholars Press, 1983), 31. See also Bernard C. Lategan, "Coming to Grips with the Reader", *Semeia* 48 (1989): 3-17.

[24] See, for instance, the way in which William S. Kurz, "Narrative Models for Imitation in Luke-Acts", in *Greeks, Romans, and Christians*, eds. David L. Balch, Everett Ferguson & Wayne A. Meeks, (Minneapolis: Fortress, 1990), 173-174, describes the implied reader:

> Because writers compose in the absence of their readers, they must imagine readers' concerns and how they would react to what is being written, unlike oral storytellers, who can adjust to listeners' actual reactions. Implied readers are the kinds of readers who are imagined or expected by the writers, and they therefore influence the way in which the text is expressed and can be reconstructed from the text itself.

[25] The way in which literary critics such as Wolfgang Iser and Umberto Eco describe the reading process can be helpful for understanding this approach to the implied reader. See Wolfgang Iser, *The Act of Reading: A Theory of Aesthetic Response* (Baltimore: Johns Hopkins University Press, 1978) and Umberto Eco, *The Role of the Reader. Explorations in the Semiotics of the Text* (London: Hutchinson, 1979).

[26] "Reader", 27.

[27] *First Kiss*, 34.

[28] Ibid., 35. See also Francis J. Moloney, "Who is 'the Reader' in/of the Fourth Gospel?", *ABR* 40

(1992): 21:
> The implied reader, therefore, is not a person but a heuristic device used to trace the temporal flow of the narrative. The reader emerges as a forward-looking textual effect who also knows and recalls what has happened and has been revealed in the story so far.

CHAPTER TWO

NARRATOR AND NARRATEE

Defining the narrator and the narratee

As soon as we start reading a narrative text, we (the real readers) become part of a narrative communication situation in which we "listen to" a voice or teller within the text telling the story. This "voice" within the text is called the *narrator*. It is important to realize that the narrator is a device that is controlled by the implied reader and, that, accordingly, it can be manipulated in various ways by the implied author. Furthermore, in all narrative texts there also will be one or more persons within the text to whom the narrator tells his/her story. This intratextual listener(s) is called the *narratee*.[1]

Apart from the fact that the narrator's presence can be deduced from the fact that someone is telling the story within the text, there are also other indicators that should be mentioned. For example, any first-person pronoun that does not designate one of the characters within the narrated world, refers to the narrator. Furthermore, if a narrative text is scrutinized thoroughly, one usually will find that certain deictic terms (such as "now", "then", "in those days", "there", etc.) are sometimes used in such a way that they do not refer to the narrated world, but to the situation from which the narration is performed. Accordingly, the existence of such a spatio-chronological situation from which the story is narrated can serve as an indication of the presence of a narrator.

In the case of the narratee more or less the same holds true. A second-person pronoun that does not refer to a character(s) within the narrated world, usually refers to the narratee. Sometimes a first-person plural may be used to indicate both the narrator and the narratee. Furthermore, the presence of explanations referring to the narratee's knowledge or attitude serves as an indication of the presence of the narratee.[2]

In order to illustrate the ways in which the presence of a narrator and narratee is indicated in a text, a few examples will be discussed:[3]

Genesis 32:32

Therefore to this day the Israelites do not eat the thigh muscle that is on the hip socket, because he struck Jacob on the hip socket at the thigh muscle.

In this example there is clearly a temporal distance between the time of narration ("this day") and the time at which the events that are narrated, occurred. This temporal distance implies a narrative situation that differs from the spatio-chronological situation of the narrated world, which in turn implies the presence of "someone" telling the story from this location, namely the narrator.

2 Samuel 13:18a

Now she (Tamar) was wearing a long robe with sleeves; for this is how the virgin daughters of the king were clothed in earlier times.

In this example we have two indications that are important. Firstly, the words "in earlier times" indicate a distance between the time of narration and the chronological setting of the narrated world, thus suggesting the presence of a narrator. Secondly, the fact that it is necessary to explain the reason why Tamar wore a long robe with sleeves indicates the presence of a hearer within the text that (supposedly) does not have this knowledge - an indication of the presence of the narratee.

Luke 1:1-4

> Since many have undertaken to set down an orderly account of the events that have been fulfilled among us, just as they were handed on to us by those who from the beginning were eyewitnesses and servants of the word, I too decided, after investigating everything carefully from the very first, to write an orderly account for you, most excellent Theophilus, so that you may know the truth concerning the things about which you have been instructed.

In this example there are several indications that are important. Firstly, as in the two previous examples, there is a temporal distance between the time of narration and the spatio-chronological setting of the narrated world. Secondly, the word "I" does not refer to any character within the narrative world, but to someone external to it, namely the narrator. Thirdly, the presence of a listener within the narrative text (narratee) is indicated not only by the personal pronoun "you", referring to a person who is not a character in the narrated world, but also by mentioning the name of this person, "Theophilus".

A typology of narrators and narratees

As indicated above, both narrator and narratee are intratextual devices that can be manipulated by the implied author in various ways. In order to give a precise description of the way in which an implied author uses a particular narrator or narratee, the following aspects should be analyzed:[4]

Temporal relations

This aspect concerns the relationship between the process of narration and the story that is being narrated. In other words, the question that should be asked is: "When did the events that are narrated occur and when are they narrated?" Four types of relationships can be identified:

* If the story is narrated *after* the events took place, it is called *ulterior narration*.
* If the story is narrated *before* the events take place, it is called *anterior*

narration.

* If the story is narrated *simultaneously* with the events that are being narrated, it is called *simultaneous narration*.

* If the act of narration and the events that are being narrated alternate, it is called *intercalated* narration.

In the case of Biblical narratives, the dominant pattern is one of *ulterior narration*, that is, the narrative is narrated after the events took place. In fact, I am not aware of any exceptions in this regard. It should be noted, though, that in some Biblical narratives events are forecasted in the story world that have not yet occurred at the time of narration. For example, in the Gospels in the New Testament the return of Jesus was still expected at the time of narration (and even now). However, this cannot be used as an argument for classifying the narration as *anterior narration*, since the prophecies in which the return of Jesus was prophesied, and which are reported by the narrator, were in themselves events that chronologically took place *before* the act of narration.

Narrative levels

It is also important to realize that a story may be told within a story. In such a case the characters in the first story (the so-called "primary" story) are used as embedded narrator(s) and narratee(s). In order to distinguish clearly between the levels on which the various narrators and narratees are employed, the following distinctions are used: The narrator and narratee on the primary level of narration are called the *extradiegetic narrator(s)/narratee(s)*, whereas the embedded narrator(s) and narratee(s) are called *intradiegetic narrator(s)/narratee(s)*. If another set of speakers and listeners are embedded within this level, they are called *hypodiegetic narrator(s)/narratees*.

In the case of such an embedded narration, it can be very useful to try to discern the function of the embedded narrative in terms of the rest of the narrative. For example, it may have an *explicative function* in that it explains something on the diegetic level. It may also have a *thematic function* in the sense that the embedded narrative may be similar or contrastive to what is being narrated on the diegetic level.

The following two examples will illustrate the use of various narrative levels in Biblical narratives:

2 Samuel 11:27b-12:5

But the thing that David had done displeased the Lord, and the Lord sent Nathan to David. He came to him, and said to him, "There were two men in a certain city, the one rich and the other poor. The rich man had very many flocks and herds; but the poor man had nothing but one little ewe lamb, which he had bought. He brought it up, and it grew up with him and with his children; it used to eat of his meager fare, and drink from his cup, and lie in his bosom, and it was like a daughter to him. Now there came a traveler to the rich man, and he was loath to take one of his own flock or herd to prepare for the wayfarer who had come to him, but he took the poor man's lamb, and prepared that for the guest who had come to him."

In this example the italic words indicate the part in which the extradiegetic narrator of this narrative is busy narrating. In the rest of the text the implied author replaces the extradiegetic narrator with Nathan, a character in the narrated world, who is used as narrator. Accordingly, Nathan can be called an intradiegetic narrator. Furthermore, David serves as the listener within this embedded narrative and thus becomes the intradiegetic narratee.

Mark 12:1-12

<u>Then he (Jesus) began to speak to them in parables.</u> *"A man planted a vineyard, put a fence around it, dug a pit for the wine press, and built a watchtower; then he leased it to tenants and went to another country. When the season came, he sent a slave to the tenants to collect from them his share of the produce of the vineyard. But they seized him, and beat him, and sent him away empty-handed. And again he sent another slave to them; this one they beat over the head and insulted. Then he sent another, and that one they killed. And so it was with many others; some they beat, and others they killed. He had still one other, a beloved son. Finally he sent him to them, saying,* <u>'They will respect my son.'</u> *But those tenants said to one another,* <u>'This is the heir; come, let us kill him, and the inheritance will be ours.'</u> *So they seized him, killed him, and threw him out of the vineyard. What then will the owner of the vineyard do? He will come*

> *and destroy the tenants and give the vineyard to others. Have you not read this scripture: 'The stone that the builders rejected has become the cornerstone; this was the Lord's doing, and it is amazing in our eyes'?"* <u>When they realized that he had told this parable against them, they wanted to arrest him, but they feared the crowd. So they left him and went away.</u>

In this example we have three narrative levels. The words underlined once indicate those parts in which the implied author uses the extradiegetic narrator. The words in italics indicate the parts in which the implied author uses Jesus, one of the characters in the narrated world, as an intradiegetic narrator. On this level the chief priests, the scribes, and the elders (see Mark 11:27) are the intradiegetic narratees. The words underlined twice indicate those parts in which Jesus, as intradiegetic narrator, uses the characters in the narrative world narrated by him as speakers and they, consequently, function on a hypodiegetic level.

Furthermore, the last two sentences in this example illustrate the point that it is useful to try to establish the function of the embedded narrative in relation to the primary narrative. In this case it is easy to determine the function of the embedded narrative, since the implied author uses the narrator in the last two sentences to point out that Jesus told the parable "against them". Accordingly it can be said that the embedded narrative has a thematic function, since its plot is similar to that of the primary narrative. However, you should note that, in most cases, the function of the embedded narrative is not indicated as explicitly as in this example and therefore you have to determine it by means of careful analysis.

Extent of participation in the story

Both the narrator and the narratee may be either absent from or present in the narrated world as characters. In the case of absent narrators and narratees, we use the term "heterodiegetic". On the other hand, if the narrator/narratee is present in the story that is being narrated (s)he is called a "homodiegetic" narrator/narratee.

In the case of Biblical narrative the dominant pattern is the use of heterodiegetic narrators and narratees. For Biblical scholars it is important to realize that the decision whether a narrator and narratee are heterodiegetic or homodiegetic must be based on the *internal evidence* of the text itself. In order to be classified as a homodiegetic narrator, the narrator should *clearly* link him/herself to one of the characters in the texts. This decision cannot be based on external evidence. For example, it cannot be argued that since Moses is the real author of Exodus (*sic!*) and since he is a character in the narrative world in Exodus, we have an example of Moses being a homodiegetic narrator in Exodus.

However, there are some examples of the use of homodiegetic narrators in Biblical narratives. For instance, the book Nehemiah begins as follows:

> The words of Nehemiah son of Hacaliah. In the month of Chislev, in the twentieth year, while I was in Susa the capital, one of my brothers, Hanani, came with certain men from Judah; and I asked them about the Jews that survived, those who had escaped the captivity, and about Jerusalem ...

In this example the narrator is linked clearly to a character in the narrated world. This relationship is maintained further on. Accordingly we can classify the narrator of Nehemiah as homodiegetic. In the case of the New Testament a homodiegetic narrator can be indicated in certain parts of the book Acts.

Degree of perceptibility

As indicated above, all narrative texts always have a narrator and a narratee. However, there can be tremendous difference regarding the way in which their perceptibility is manifested in the text. In this regard we can speak of a continuum ranging from a maximum of covertness to a maximum of overtness. In order to decide on how the perceptibility of a certain narrator should be classified, the following can be used as criteria:

* Description of setting
* Identification of characters
* Temporal summaries

* Description of characters/events
* Reports of what the characters did not think or say
* Commentary

In the case of an overt narrator his/her presence in the text will be very clear due to a large number of some or all of the above-mentioned aspects. In the case of a covert narrator the opposite is the case. Furthermore it is important to note that the degree of perceptibility of the narrator/narratee may vary considerably within the same narrative.

In the case of Biblical narratives it is difficult to indicate a general trend, since the perceptibility of the narrator often differs from chapter to chapter. My impression is that, in general, the Biblical narrator is fairly perceptible. However, there certainly are exceptions where the narrator's perceptibility can be classified as maximum covert - especially in those parts where extensive monologues or dialogues are reported. For example, in the Sermon on the Mount (Matthew 5-7) and in the Farewell Discourses and Prayer of Farewell (John 13:31-17:26) the narrator's presence is only perceptible in a few introductory words.

Reliability

It is also possible to classify narrators and narratees in terms of their reliability. Due to the fact that the narratees are almost continuously covert in Biblical narrative, I shall concentrate on the signs of reliability/un-reliability of the narrator.[5] To determine whether a narrator is reliable or not, the following can serve as guidelines: If it becomes clear that a narrator only has limited knowledge of the events that s/he narrates, s/he may be unreliable. Furthermore, if it becomes clear that a narrator is involved personally in the story s/he narrates to such an extent that the narrative is deliberately distorted to suit a particular purpose, s/he may be classified as unreliable. Lastly, if there is a definite clash between the value systems of the narrator and the implied author, the narrator can be classified as unreliable.

If we turn to Biblical narrators, I tend to agree with Meir Sternberg's[6] statement that the narrators in the Hebrew Bible are "straightforwardly reliable". It seems to me as if this also holds true for the narrators in the New Testament. In any case, one would not expect the use of unreliable narrators in narrative texts that have such strong ideological (or theological) overtones as is the case in Biblical narratives, since this would undermine their rhetorical effectiveness.

However, we should also take note of the important remarks of David Gunn and Danna Fewell[7] with regard to the reliability of narrators in the Hebrew Bible: Due to the intricate and complex way in which many parts of the Hebrew Bible developed, we often are confronted with a final text at odds with itself. For example, in terms of the factuality of the narrated world, it could be asked: "Who did kill Goliath?" (see 1 Samuel 17 and 2 Samuel 21:19) or "Just when did the tribes of Israel take possession of the land?" (see Joshua 10-12 and Judges 1). Thus, although the individual narrators of individual narratives in, say, Genesis - 2 Kings, can all be classified as reliable, when we posit a single narrator for Genesis - 2 Kings, the reliability of the narrator may become a problem.

The functions of a narrator

The last issue to be highlighted is the various functions that a narrator may fulfill in a narrative.[8] Apart from narrating the story, the following three functions that a narrator may fulfill are important if narratology is used as an exegetic tool:

* *Directing function*: This function is fulfilled when a narrator makes meta-narrative remarks, that is remarks concerning the internal organization of the narrative. This can be achieved, for example, by indicating articulations, connections or interrelationships within the narrative text.

In order to illustrate this function in Biblical narrative, the following two examples from the Fourth Gospel can be cited:

John 2:11

Jesus did this, the first of his signs, in Cana of Galilee, and revealed his glory ...

John 4:54

Now this was the second sign that Jesus did after coming from Judea to Galilee.

In both cases the narrator is fulfilling a directing function. By counting the signs, the narrator draws attention to one of the important aspects in the overall organization of this Gospel, namely the fact that only seven signs are narrated.

* *Ideological function*: The implied author may use the narrator to explicitly voice the ideological perspective that it wants to communicate to the implied reader. Many exegetes who use narratology in exegesis identify this as "point of view" - which, however, is an unfortunate choice. (This will be discussed fully in the next chapter.) I prefer the use of the term ideological (or even theological) perspective. What is important to note, however, is that the use of the narrator to voice the ideological perspective explicitly is but one option that the implied author has for communicating the ideological perspective to the implied reader. Other options that can be used are the way in which the plot is construed, interaction between characters, juxtaposition of scenes, etc.

In order to illustrate the way in which this function may be fulfilled by narrators in the Bible, the following two examples can be cited:

2 Kings 23:25

Before him (= Josiah) there was no king like him, who turned to the Lord with all his heart, with all his soul, and with all his might, according to all the laws of Moses; nor did any like him arise after him.

John 20:30-31

Now Jesus did many other signs in the presence of his disciples, which are not written in this book. But these are written so that you may come to believe that Jesus is the Messiah, the Son of God, and that through believing you may have life in his name.

In both cases the implied author uses the narrator to convey the ideological perspective in a rather explicit way. In the case of 2 Kings 23:25 the implied author's perception with regard to way in which one should behave towards God can be deduced easily from the way in which the conduct of king Josiah is evaluated. In the case of John 20:31 the ideological perspective conveyed by the narrator concerns the identity of Jesus (He is regarded as the Messiah and the Son of God) and the reaction expected from the implied reader (belief).

* *Testimonial function*: This function (also called the function of attestation) refers to the relationship (affective, moral or intellectual) that the narrator has to the story s/he tells. The narrator can fulfill this function in various ways, for example, by indicating the sources of his/her information, the degree of precision of his/her memories, or the feelings that the story (or a part of it) awakens in him/her.

In the case of Biblical narrative one of the best examples of the function of attestation is the first verses of the Gospel of Luke, already quoted in this chapter. The function of attestation is also fulfilled in John 21:24 where the Beloved Disciple is indicated as the source (and real author?) of the Gospel.[9] In the case of the Hebrew Bible we have several examples where the narrator cites works in which additional material can be found, for example 1 Kings 11:41; 14:19; 14:29; and 2 Chronicles 27:7 and 28:26. However, since it is not clear whether these sources were also used in the compilation of these narratives, these examples cannot be classified with absolute certainty as cases of attestation.

Before concluding this chapter I wish to point out that the distinctions provided in it should never be seen as an end in itself. The identification and classification of narrators and narratees, as well as the analysis of the functions they fulfill, are important issues that are best described in terms of a rigid framework such as the one presented above, since this enables one to pinpoint possible differences between various narratives. However, if this has all been done, one should not rest content. It is important to use this as a starting point to go further in the sense that one should also scrutinize the narrative to establish whether it is possible to determine other significant features from the way in which narrator and narratee are employed in the text. I shall illustrate this by means of two examples.

Following the distinctions provided above, the narrator in the *Book of Jonah* can be described as follows: The story is narrated by means of ulterior narration by an extradiegetic narrator to an extradiegetic narratee, but quite often the characters in the narrative world (for example, God, Jonah and the sailors) are used as intradiegetic speakers and hearers. Furthermore, both narrator and narratee can be classified as heterodiegetic, since they are not characters in the narrated world. Whereas the narratee's perceptibility can be classified as a maximum of covertness, the narrator's perceptibility varies from being fairly perceptible (for example, Jonah 1:1-6) to a maximum of covertness (for example, Jonah 2:1-9). The narrator can also be classified as reliable, since there is no evidence to the contrary. Furthermore, there are no conspicuous examples of the narrator fulfilling any of the functions outlined above. One could rest content with everything mentioned so far, since it gives a fairly good description of both narrator and narratee in the Book of Jonah. However, further analysis can be worthwhile. For example, Kenneth M. Craig[10] points out several interesting features with regard to the narrator in the Book of Jonah. To mention but a few: The paratactic style and the lack of subordinate clauses in the narrator's style highlight the quick pace of the story; the words used by the narrator in describing the activity of the Lord (He "appoints" a great fish to swallow Jonah [1:17] and later "speaks" to the fish causing it to spew Jonah out upon dry land [2:10]) emphasize that he, as the creator God, is in full control; and, lastly, very interesting patterns can be discerned in terms of the relationship between narration and dialogue: in some cases (for example, 1:7a and 1:7b; 1:12a and 1:15a) narration confirms dialogue whereas the opposite pattern is also used (1:4 and 1:11a; 3:5 and 3:8a).

As a second example the way in which narrator and narratee are employed in the Gospel of Luke will be considered. In terms of the criteria outlined above, I shall classify the narrator and narratee in the Gospel of Luke as follows: The implied author uses a reliable,[11] extradiegetic, heterodiegetic narrator who narrates the story by means of ulterior narration and whose perceptibility varies between being fairly perceptible and covert. The implied author often uses embedded narrators and narratees, for example Jesus, the disciples and the other characters. The narratee can also be classified as extradiegetic and heterodiegetic. His perceptibility can almost always be classified as a maximum of covertness. A notable exception, however, is Luke 1:1-4 where his presence is not only indicated by means of a direct address, but also by citing his name (Theophilus).

Apart from what has been indicated so far, it is also possible to discover other subtleties in the way in which the narrator is employed. For example, James Dawsey[12] indicates the following: The voice of the narrator in the Gospel of Luke is an affected one in the sense that his/her narration is characterized by the repetition of certain Septuagintal formulas. Furthermore it is clear that the implied author considered aspects such as proper sound, harmony and rhythm when formulating the narrator's speech. Dawsey also indicates that the locus of the narrator's language is the community of faith: the story that is related belongs to and is directed to people who worship Jesus. Another interesting aspect indicated by Dawsey is that there is a significant difference between the speech of Jesus (as character) and the speech of the narrator. In contrast to the narrator Jesus speaks in a popular style, using the language of common people.

Suggestions for further reading on the theoretical aspects of narrator and narratee

Bal, Mieke. *Narratology. Introduction to the Theory of Narrative*. Toronto: University of Toronto Press, 1985: 120-125; 134-155.
Chatman, Seymour. *Story and Discourse. Narrative Structure in Fiction and Film*. Ithaca: Cornell, 1978: 147-260.
Cohan, Steven, & Shires, Linda M. *Telling Stories. A Theoretical Analysis of Narrative Fiction*. New York: Routledge, 1988: 89-92.
Genette, Gérard. *Narrative Discourse*. Oxford: Basil Blackwell, 1980: 11-262.
Genette, Gérard. *Narrative Discourse Revisited*. Ithaca: Cornell University Press, 1988: 79-134.
Prince, Gerald. *A Dictionary of Narratology*. University of Nebraska Press, 1987.
Prince, Gerald. "Introduction to the Study of the Narratee", in *Narratology. An Introduction*, eds. Susana Onega & José Angel García Landa, (London: Longman, 1996), 190-202.
Prince, Gerald. *Narratology. The Form and Functioning of Narrative*. Berlin: Mouton, 1982: 7-25.
Prince, Gerald. "Notes toward a Categorization of Fictional Narratees", *Genre* 4/1 (1971): 100-106.
Rimmon-Kenan, Shlomith. *Narrative Fiction. Contemporary Poetics*. London: Metheuen, 1983: 86-116.
Stanzel, Franz K. *A Theory of Narrative*. Cambridge: Cambridge University Press, 1984: 46-62; 248-250.

Suggestions for further reading on narrator and narratee in Biblical narratives

Amit, Yairah. "'The Glory of Israel Does Not Deceive or Change His Mind': On the Reliability of Narrators and Speakers in Biblical Narrative", *Prooftexts* 12 (1992): 201-212.
Bar-Efrat, Shimon. *Narrative Art in the Bible*. Sheffield: Almond, 1989: 13-46.
Berlin, Adele. *Poetics and Interpretation of Biblical Narrative*. Sheffield: Almond, 1983: 43-82.
Caspi, Michael Maswari. "The Story of the Rape of Dinah: The Narrator and the Reader", *HebStud* 26/1 (1985): 25-45.
Creech, R. Robert. "The Most Excellent Narratee: The Significance of Theophilus in Luke-Acts", in *With Steadfast Purpose. Essays on Acts in Honor of Henry Jackson Flanders Jr.*, ed. Naymond H. Keathley, (Waco: Baylor University Press, 1990), 107-127.
Culpepper, R. Alan. *Anatomy of the Fourth Gospel. A Study in Literary Design*. Philadelphia: Fortress, 1983: 13-50; 205-211.
Dawsey, James M. *The Lukan Voice: Confusion and Irony in the Gospel of Luke*. Macon: Mercer University Press, 1986.
Deist, Ferdinand. "A Note on the Narrator's Voice in Genesis 37, 20-22," *ZAW* 108/4 (1996): 621-622.
Eslinger, Lyle. *Into the Hands of the Living God*. Sheffield: Almond Press, 1980.
Fowler, Robert M. *Let the Reader Understand. Reader-Response Criticism and the Gospel of Mark*. Minneapolis: Fortress, 1991: 61-154.
Funk, Robert W. *The Poetics of Biblical Narrative*. Sonoma: Polebridge, 1988: 29-33.
Gunn, David M. & Fewell, Danna Nolan. *Narrative in the Hebrew Bible*. Oxford: Oxford University Press, 1993: 52-62.

Gunn, David M. "Reading Right. Reliable and Omniscient Narrator, Omniscient God, and Foolproof Composition in the Hebrew Bible" in *The Bible in Three Dimensions. Essays in Celebration of Forty Years of Biblical Studies in the University of Sheffield*, eds. David J. A. Clines, Stephen E. Fowl and Stanley E. Porter, (Sheffield: Sheffield Academic Press, 1990), 53-64.
Hedrick, Charles, W. "Narrator and Story in the Gospel of Mark: Hermeneia and Paradosis", *PRSt* 14 (1987): 239-258.
Kurz, William S. "Effects of Variant Narrators in Acts 10-11", *NTS* 43 (1997): 570-586.
Moore, Stephen D. *Literary Criticism and the Gospels*. New Haven: Yale, 1989: 25-40.
Sheeley, Steven. "The Narrator in the Gospels: Developing a Model", *PRSt* 16 (1989): 213-223.
Staley, Jeffrey L. *The Print's First Kiss: A Rhetorical Investigation of the Implied Reader in the Fourth Gospel*. Atlanta: Scholars Press, 1988: 37-46.
Sternberg, Meir. *The Poetics of Biblical Narrative. Ideological Literature and the Drama of Reading*. Bloomington: Indiana University Press, 1985: 84-128; 153-185.
Tolmie, D. Francois. "John 21:24-25: A Case of Failed Attestation?", *Skrif en Kerk* 17/2 (1996): 420-426.
White, Hugh C. *Narration and Discourse in the Book of Genesis*. Cambridge: Cambridge University Press, 1991: 95-106.

Notes

[1] For more technical definitions of "narrator" and "narratee", see Bal, *Narratology*, 119, and Gerald Prince, *Narratology. The Form and Functioning of Narrative* (Berlin: Mouton, 1982), 16-25.
[2] See Prince, *Narratology*, 8-10 and 17-29, for a detailed discussion.
[3] For more examples, see Sternberg, *Poetics*, 120-121, and Bar-Efrat, *Narrative Art*, 19-45.
[4] The following discussion is based on Rimmon-Kenan, *Narrative Fiction*, 89-105, who follows Genette and Chatman.
[5] See Chatman, *Story and Discourse*, 260-261, for a discussion of the unreliable narratee.
[6] *Poetics*, 51. See also Yairah Amit, "'The Glory of Israel Does Not Deceive or Change His Mind': On the Reliability of Narrator and Speakers in Biblical Narrative", *Prooftexts* 12 (1992): 201-212, who indicates that only God and the narrator always appear as reliable in the Hebrew Bible.
[7] David M. Gunn & Danna Nolan Fewell, *Narrative in the Hebrew Bible* (Oxford: Oxford University Press, 1993), 53-56.
[8] This discussion is based on Genette, *Narrative Discourse*, 255-259.
[9] It seems as if the awkward manner in which the function of attestation is fulfilled in John 21:24-25 undermines its intended effect. See D. Francois Tolmie, "John 21:24-25: A Case of Failed Attestation?", *Skrif en Kerk* 17/2 (1996): 420-426.
[10] *A Poetics of Jonah* (Columbia: University of South Columbia, 1993), 45-58.
[11] On this issue see Robert C. Tannehill, *The Narrative Unity of Luke-Acts. A Literary Interpretation. Volume One: The Gospel according to Luke* (Philadelphia: Fortress, 1986), 6-7 - in particular note 4 on page 7.
[12] James M. Dawsey, *The Lukan Voice. Confusion and Irony in the Gospel of Luke* (Macon: Mercer University Press, 1986), 15-42.

CHAPTER THREE

FOCALIZATION

Focalization or point of view?

In the discussion of narrative texts scholars usually pay a fair amount of attention to what they call "point of view". Due to the influential studies of eminent scholars such as Percy Lubbock,[1] Cleanth Brooks & Robert Penn Warren,[2] Franz K. Stanzel,[3] Norman Friedman[4] and Wayne C. Booth[5] the study of point view has become part and parcel of nearly all the formulated theories of narrative.[6] Unfortunately this concept is not always used by scholars in the same way and this situation leads to confusion. Broadly speaking, the concept "point of view" is usually linked to the various perspectives from which a narrative may be told. In this regard the ways in which the concept "point of view" is used - not only by scholars in general, but also by Biblical scholars[7] - are usually influenced in one way or another by the following three frameworks:

Brooks and Warren[8] identify four ways in which the "focus of narration" can be manipulated:

    1. First person: the main character tells his/her own story himself/herself.
    2. First-person observer: a minor character tells the main character's story.

3. Author-observer: an author tells the story as an observer.

4. Omniscient author: an analytic or omniscient author tells the story.

Secondly, the narrative situations distinguished by Franz K. Stanzel[9] should be mentioned:

1. Authorial narrative situation: an omniscient author tells the story.

2. First-person narrator: one of the characters is used as narrator and tells the story in the first person.

3. Personal narration: a narrative is narrated in such a way that the reader gets the impression that s/he views the events through the eyes of one of the characters.

A third study that is often used is that of Boris Uspensky[10] who distinguishes the following "planes" in point of view:

* *Ideological plane*: The point of view assumed by a narrator when s/he evaluates a narrative world ideologically.

* *Phraseological plane*: The point of view manifested in the diction used by a narrator or by the way in which speech is used in a text.

* *Spatial* and *temporal planes*: The spatial and temporal co-ordinates from which the narrated world is presented.

* *Psychological plane*: The consciousness which is used in order to present events. This may vary from a deliberately chosen subjective position, to a point of view chosen as objectively as possible.

In most studies of Biblical narrative in which you will find the concept "point of view", it will be influenced in one way or another by the distinctions outlined above. However, because the concept is used in so many different ways, it will be necessary to make sure exactly what is meant when it is employed. If you decide to use the concept yourself, I suggest that you provide a definition in order to clarify what you mean by it.

In this book I shall be following a group of narratologists who prefer not to use the concept "point of view" at all. This is largely due to the fact that Gérard Genette pointed out some weak spots in the way in which the concept "point of view" is handled by scholars. In *Narrative Discourse*[11] he makes the important observation that a confusion between two questions, namely "Who is the narrator?" and "Who is the character whose point of view orients the narrative perspective?" can be discerned in the traditional approach to narrative.[12] In other words, the questions "Who speaks?" and "Who perceives?" are confused in the traditional approach to point of view. Of course, in many narrative texts "speaking" and "narrating" can be attributed to the same agent, but this need not be the case, and accordingly it is a theoretical necessity to distinguish between them. This distinction becomes clear when one compares what happens in a narrative text with what happens in a film or television. In a film the narrator that tells the story (if there is one) is not to be confused with the way in which the vision is manipulated (the place from which the camera shoots the story). The same kind of distinction can be made in narrative texts, since in a narrative text there is a voice that tells the story (the narrator), but the story is also "viewed" through the eyes of an onlooker or through the eyes of one of the characters - the so-called locus of perception. Genette argues that this distinction is not accounted for in the traditional approach to point of view. For example, according to the traditional approach to point of view, scholars cannot describe accurately what happens in a narrative text if the narrator is changed, but the locus of perception is not changed, or when the locus of perception is changed, but the narrator is not changed. In order to clarify these aspects, he introduces the concept "focalization" and makes a distinction between the voice that tells the story, that is, the narrator (as discussed in the previous chapter in this book) and "focalization". "Focalization" is then restricted to the way in which the vision (the "camera") is manipulated in a narrative text. Thus, to put it simply: in order to analyze focalization in a narrative text, we should ask the question: Through whose eyes do we view the events that are being narrated to us?

Procedures for analyzing focalization

In order to analyze the way in which focalization is handled in a Biblical narrative, the following two distinctions are useful:[13]

1. Locus of focalization

In this regard one should distinguish between two possible types of focalization: In the case of *external focalization* the locus of focalization is external to the story. In this case the events that are narrated, are presented in such a way that it seems as if they are perceived ("viewed") by an onlooker who does not play any role in the story himself/herself. In *internal focalization* the events are narrated in such a way that it seems as if they are perceived through the eyes of one of the characters in the narrative. Note that the locus of focalization can be varied in the same narrative.

In order to understand the distinction between external and internal focalization it may be helpful for you to think of the way in which the camera (the locus of perception) may be manipulated in the movies or on television. In some cases the camera is placed in such a way that it functions as an impersonal onlooker, thus being a case of external focalization. In other cases the camera can be placed in such a way that it seems as if we are perceiving the story through the eyes of one of the characters (internal focalization) - a technique used quite often in horror movies.

2. The focalized object(s)

It is also important to analyze the way in which the focalized objects, that is, the characters, are perceived in the narrative text. Once again we can distinguish between two possibilities: In some cases characters can be focalized only *externally*, that is, only the outward manifestations of the character are portrayed. In the case of *internal focalization of the focalized*, the inner feelings, knowledge and thoughts of the characters are portrayed.

Examples from Biblical narrative

In order to illustrate the way in which focalization is used in Biblical writings I shall discuss a few examples. The first example comes from the Hebrew Bible. In 1 Samuel 1:1-28 the story of Samuel's birth in answer to prayer is narrated. I shall discuss the second scene (verses 9-18) where Hannah visits the temple.

> (9) After they had eaten and drunk at Shiloh, Hannah rose and presented herself before the Lord. Now Eli the priest was sitting on the seat beside the doorpost of the temple of the Lord. (10) <u>She was deeply distressed</u> and prayed to the Lord, and wept bitterly. (11) She made this vow: "O Lord of Hosts, if only you will look on the misery of your servant, and remember me, and not forget your servant, but will give to your servant a male child, then I will set him before you as a nazirite until the day of his death. He shall drink neither wine nor intoxicants, and no razor shall touch his head." (12) As she continued praying before the Lord, Eli observed her mouth. (13) *Hannah was praying silently; only her lips moved, but her voice was not heard;* <u>therefore Eli thought she was drunk</u>. (14) So Eli said to her, "How long will you make a drunken spectacle of yourself? Put away your wine." (15) But Hannah answered, "No, my lord, I am a woman deeply troubled; I have drunk neither wine nor strong drink, but I have been pouring my soul out before the Lord. (16) Do not regard your servant as a worthless woman, for I have been speaking out my great anxiety and vexation all the time." (17) Then Eli answered, "Go in peace; the God of Israel grant the petition you have made to him." (18) And she said, "Let your servant find favor in your sight." Then the woman went to her quarters, ate and drank with her husband, and her countenance was sad no longer.

This example illustrates three aspects of focalization:

1. The *locus of focalization* is situated externally almost throughout. The events are portrayed as if perceived by an onlooker from a distance. However, there is one exception. In verse 13 (printed in italics in the quotation above) the locus of focalization is moved to an internal position, since the events are now portrayed as they are perceived through the eyes of Eli. Note that although there

is a change in focalization, there is no change in narrator - thus illustrating the fact that Genette's emphasis on making a distinction between focalization and narration is vital. From verse 14 onwards the locus of focalization is once again located externally.

2. It is rather interesting to note the movement between the two *focalized objects*, Hannah and Eli. The focus moves back and forth between these two characters:

>9a: Hannah
>9b: Eli
>10-11: Hannah
>12: Eli
>13a: Hannah (through Eli's eyes)
>13b-14: Eli
>15-16: Hannah
>17: Eli
>18: Hannah.

3. The focalized objects (Hannah and Eli) are mostly focalized externally only. There are, however, two exceptions (underlined in the quotation above). In verse 10a Hannah's emotions are focalized and in verse 13c Eli's inner thoughts are focalized.

For the analysis of focalization in the Hebrew Bible it is useful to take note of the following observation: Adele Berlin[14] indicates that the Hebrew word *hinneh* (look!) is often used to indicate a shift in focalization in narratives in the Hebrew Bible. Consider Judges 4:22 where it is narrated what happened when Jael went out of his tent to meet Barak:

>And *hinneh* Barak was pursuing Sisera ... and he came to her and *hinneh* Sisera was fallen dead with a tent peg in his temple (Berlin's translation).

In this case the first *hinneh* changes the focalization from inside Jael's tent to the outside where Barak is coming into view. The second *hinneh* switches the locus of focalization from Jael's perspective to that of Barak.

With regard to internal focalization of the focalized in Biblical narratives it should be noted that although such examples are found quite often, they are usually done briefly without any long discussion of inner emotional turmoil or struggle. The following examples will illustrate this:

Gen 38:15

When Judah saw her (Tamar), he thought her to be a prostitute...

2 Kings 13:19

Then the man of God (Elisha) was angry with him, and said, "You should have struck five or six times..."

Matthew 2:3

When King Herod heard this, he was frightened, and all Jerusalem with him...

Mark 6:51-52

Then he (Jesus) got into the boat with them and the wind ceased. And they (the disciples) were utterly astounded, for they did not understand about the loaves, but their hearts were hardened.

John 13:2

The devil had already put it into the heart of Judas son of Simon Iscariot to betray him.

In the New Testament an interesting example of the movement of focus is found in John 18:12-27 (Jesus before the Jewish authorities). Although the locus of focalization (external "onlooker"-focalization) remains the same throughout, there is a movement in the way in which the focalized objects are presented. In John 18:12-14 the events before Annas, the father-in-law of Caiaphas, are portrayed. The focalized objects are thus perceived as being *inside*. In verses 15-18 the focus shifts to the *outside*. The focalized objects are Peter, the other disciple (the beloved disciple?) and the woman guarding the gate. She asks Peter whether he is a disciple of Jesus, but he denies it. In verses 19-24 the focus shifts back to the *inside* where Jesus is questioned by the Jewish authorities. Jesus is portrayed as answering the questions boldly and even aggressively. In verses 25-27 the focus shifts back to the *outside* where Peter denies being a disciple of Jesus for the second and third time. The movement in focalization is highly significant, since the contrast between what happens inside and what happens outside serves to portray dramatically Peter's inability to fulfill his promise to lay down his life for Jesus.

In Acts we have an interesting example where the same events (Paul's call on the road to Damascus) are narrated twice,[15] but are focalized differently.[16] In Acts 9:1-18 the events are focalized *externally*, that is, the locus of focalization is situated in such a way that the events are portrayed as if viewed by an impersonal onlooker. In Acts 22:6-16 the same events are narrated, but in this case the implied author uses Paul as an embedded narrator. Accordingly the locus of focalization is changed to an *internal* position, since everything is portrayed as if viewed through Paul's eyes. Since the same events are narrated in both instances, one can indicate many similarities, such as the bright light from heaven, Jesus' question as to why Paul persecutes him, Paul's question as to Jesus' identity, the order to go to Damascus, the astonishment of Paul's companions and his blindness.

However, what is more interesting is the way in which these two accounts differ. Firstly, the change from external focalization to internal focalization means that the same events are portrayed from a different angle. This is best illustrated by comparing the two episodes in which Ananias lays his hands on Paul:

> *Acts 9:17*
> So Ananias went and entered the house. He laid his hands on Saul and said, "Brother Saul, the Lord Jesus, who appeared to you on your way here, has sent me so that you may regain your sight and be filled with the Holy Spirit". And immediately something like scales fell from his eyes, and his sight was restored...
>
> *Acts 22:12-13*
> A certain Ananias, who was a devout man according to the law and well spoken of by all the Jews living there, came to me; and standing beside me, he said, "Brother Saul, regain your sight!" In that very hour I regained my sight and saw him...

A second difference between the two accounts is that the choice of an internal locus of focalization in the second account means that the events that are portrayed should be restricted to those events that can be perceived from Paul's perspective. This means that the account of Ananias' vision in Acts 9:10-14 (in his own home?) could not be included in the second version in Acts 22, since they do not fall within Paul's (limited) perspective.

Suggestions for further reading on the analysis of focalization in narrative texts

Bal, Mieke. "The Laughing Mice, or: On Focalization", *Poetics Today* 2/2 (1981): 202-210.
Bal, Mieke. *Narratology. Introduction to the Theory of Narrative.* Toronto: University of Toronto Press, 1985: 100-115.
Berendsen, Marjet. "The Teller and the Observer: Narration and Focalization in Narrative Texts", *Style* 18/2 (1984): 140-159.
Cohan, Steven & Shires, Linda M. *Telling Stories. A Theoretical Analysis of Narrative Fiction.* New York: Routledge, 1988: 95-104.
Edminston, William F. "Focalization and the First-Person Narrator: A Revision of Theory", *Poetics Today* 10/4 (1989): 729-743.
Fowler, Roger. "How to See Through Language: Perspective in Fiction", *Poetics* 11 (1982): 213-235.
Genette, Gérard. *Narrative Discourse.* Oxford: Basil Blackwell, 1984: 185-210.
Genette, Gérard. *Narrative Discourse Revisited.* Ithaca: Cornell University Press, 1988: 64-78.
Herman, David. "Hypothetical Focalization", *Narrative* 2/3 (1994): 230-253.
Martin, Wallace. *Recent Theories of Narrative.* Ithaca: Cornell, 1986: 145-147.
Nelles, William. "Getting Focalization into Focus", *Poetics Today* 11/2 (1990): 365-382.
Prince, Gerald. *A Dictionary of Narratology.* University of Nebraska Press, 1987.
Rimmon-Kenan, Shlomith. *Narrative Fiction. Contemporary Poetics.* London: Metheuen, 1983: 71-86.

Suggestions for further reading on focalization in Biblical narratives

Berlin, Adele. *Poetics and Interpretation of Biblical Narrative.* Sheffield: Almond, 1983: 43-82.
Eslinger, Lyle. *Into the Hands of the Living God.* Sheffield: Sheffield Academic Press, 1980.
Boomershine, Thomas & Bartholomew, Gilbert. "Narrative Technique of Mark 16:8", *JBL* 100 (1981): 213-223.
Fowler, Robert M. *Let the Reader Understand. Reader-Response Criticism and the Gospel of Mark.* Minneapolis: Fortress, 1991: 66-74.
Jasper, Alison. "Interpretative Approaches to John 20:1-18: Mary at the Tomb of Jesus", *StTh* 47/2 (1993): 107-118.
Kurz, William S. *Reading Luke-Acts. Dynamics of Biblical Narrative.* Louisville: Westminster, John Knox, 1993: 111-124.
Menn, Esther Marie. *Judah and Tamar (Genesis 38) in Ancient Jewish Exegesis. Studies in Literary Form and Hermeneutics.* Leiden: E J Brill, 1997: 28-40.
Pamment, Margaret. "Focus in the Fourth Gospel", *ET* 97/3 (1985): 71-75.
Smith, Stephen H. *A Lion with Wings: A Narrative-Critical Approach to Mark's Gospel.* Sheffield: Sheffield Academic Press, 1996: 166-199.
Stibbe, Mark W. G. "A Tomb with a View: John 11:1-44 in Narrative-Critical Perspective", *NTS* 40 (1994): 35-54.

Tovey, Derek. *Narrative Art and Act in the Fourth Gospel*. Sheffield: Sheffield Academic Press, 1997.

Notes

[1] *The Craft of Fiction* (London: Garden City, 1921), 251-264.
[2] *Understanding Fiction* (New York: Appleton-Century-Crofts, 1943).
[3] *Narrative Situations in the Novel* (Bloomington: Indiana University Press, 1955. Translated from the German).
[4] "Point of view in Fiction: The Development of a Critical Concept", *PMLA* 70 (1955): 1160-1184.
[5] *Rhetoric of Fiction*.
[6] For example, Robie Macauley & George Lanning, *Technique in Fiction* (New York: Harper & Row, 1964), 99-111; Robert Stanton, *An Introduction to Fiction* (New York: Holt, Rinehart & Winston, 1965), 26-29; Robert Scholes & Robert Kellogg, *The Nature of Narrative* (Oxford: Oxford University Press, 1966), 240-282; Marjorie Boulton, *The Anatomy of the Novel* (London: Routledge & Kegan Paul, 1975), 29-44; Klaus Kanzog, *Eine Einführung in die Normeinübing des Erzählens* (Heidelberg: Quelle & Meyer, 1976), 26-29; and William C. Knott, *The Craft of Fiction* (Reston: Reston Publishing Company, 1977), 97-111.
[7] As examples the following works may be cited: Norman Petersen, "Point of View in Mark's Narrative", *Semeia* 12 (1978): 97-121; Jacob Licht, *Storytelling in the Bible* (Jerusalem: Magnes Press, 1978), 75-86; James L. Resseguie, "Point of View in the Central Section of Luke (5:51-19:44)", *JETS* 23 (1982): 41-47; Rhoads & Michie, *Mark*, 43-44; William S. Kurz, "Narrative Approaches to Luke-Acts", *Bib* 68 (1987): 204-206; Andries G. van Aarde, "Narrative Point of View: An Ideological Reading of Luke 12:35-48", *Neotest* 22/2 (1988): 235-252; Bar-Efrat, *Narrative Art*, 14-17; Fowler, *Let the Reader*, 66-72; Powell, *Narrative Criticism*, 23-25; and J. Warren Holleran, "Seeing the Light: A Narrative Reading of John 9", *EThL* 69 (1993): 24-36.
[8] *Understanding Fiction*, 588-590. Note that they prefer the term "locus of perception" to "point of view".
[9] *Typische Formen des Romans* (Göttingen: Vandenhoeck & Ruprecht, 1965), 16-17.
[10] *The Poetics of Composition. The Structure of the Artistic Text and Typology of a Compositional Form* (London: University of California Press, 1973), 8-100.
[11] *Narrative Discourse*, 161-211. Bal, *Narratology*, 100-118, follows Genette and also opts for the concept "focalization". She defines it as "the relationship between the vision, the agent that sees and that which is seen". She summarizes this relationship as follows: "A says that B sees what C is doing." See also Ernst van Alphen & Irene de Jong, eds. *Door het oog van de tekst. Essays voor Mieke Bal over visie* (Muiderberg: Dick Coutinho, 1988), for a number of essays on focalization dedicated to Bal. Also see Rimmon-Kenan, *Narrative Fiction*, 74-82; Wallace Martin, *Recent Theories of Narrative* (Ithaca: Cornell, 1986), 145-147; and Jos Dembinski, "Focalization and the First Person Narrator: A Revision of Theory", *Poetics Today* 10/4 (1989): 730-735.
[12] Genette, *Narrative Discourse*, 186-189. He discusses Lubbock, Blin, Stendhal, Brooks & Warren and Stanzel as examples in this regard.
[13] I follow the distinctions made by Rimmon-Kenan, *Narrative Fiction*, 74-77. Note that I do not include her discussion of "facets of focalization".
[14] *Poetics and Interpretation*, 43-82. This is an excellent discussion of focalization in the Hebrew Bible. Note that Berlin still uses the term "point of view". However her remarks with regard to what she calls spatial point of view come very close to what I identify as focalization.
[15] Actually they are narrated three times (See Acts 26:12-18), but, as the episode in which Ananias' role is portrayed is not recounted in the third version, it is not discussed here.
[16] The following discussion is based on that of William S. Kurz, *Reading Luke-Acts. Dynamics of Biblical Narrative* (Louisville: Westminster, 1993), 129-130.

CHAPTER FOUR

CHARACTER

If variety is the spice of life, character can be regarded as the spice of narrative! This certainly also holds true of Biblical narratives. Biblical characters such as Abraham, Moses, King David, Jesus, Peter and Paul always have been a profound source of fascination for religious people. A narratological approach to character will enable us not only to explain the various ways and means of characterization at the disposal of the implied author, but also to understand how characterization is achieved in individual narratives.

However, before turning to practical matters, it is necessary to point out that there are some points of dispute with regard to the analysis of characters amongst literary critics. The two most important points of dispute are, firstly, the relationship between characters in the text and people in the real world, and, secondly, the relationship between characters and actions in a narrative text.[1]

With regard to the first issue (the relationship between characters in texts and people in the real world) the difference of opinion can be formulated as the opposition between a "realistic" and a "purist" approach to character.[2] Literary critics who choose a "realistic" option believe that the characters in a narrative text acquire a kind of independence, and analyze and discuss them as if they were real human beings. On the other hand, literary critics opting for a "purist" approach take as their point of departure that characters can only exist insofar as they function in the events and images portrayed within the narrative text. In the discussion in this chapter I shall try to avoid being extremist in this regard, but my discussion will incline towards the "purist" approach, since I shall focus on the process of characterization. However, this does not necessarily exclude the "realistic" approach, since any real reader will inevitably perceive the reconstructed characters in the story world in terms of his/her perceptions of the factors constituting being human.

The second point of dispute (the relationship between characters and events) concerns the issue as to which of these two aspects should be subordinated to the other. There are some literary critics who claim that the characters are subordinated to the action in a narrative text. This tendency is found in the way in which character was handled in Formalistic and Structuralistic[3] approaches to narrative. For example, in his analysis of Russian folktales, Vladimir Propp[4] reduced all the characters in the Russian folktales that he analyzed to what he called seven "spheres of action". The same tendency can be illustrated in the actantial model developed by A. J. Greimas (this will be discussed further on in this chapter). However, the opposite tendency can also be found in modern theories on character. For example, Fernando Ferraro[5] views the characters in the narrative as the structuring elements in texts, and argues that all the events in a narrative text can only attain coherence and plausibility as a result of their relationship to the characters. In order to settle this issue, I wish to point out Shlomith Rimmon-Kenan's[6] views in this regard, since they seem to be a very sensible. She argues that, instead of subordinating one to the other, we should think of character and action as being interdependent. Two of her arguments are important: Firstly, we should take the type of narrative into consideration. In some narratives the action may predominate, whereas the opposite may be true in other narratives. Secondly, the reversibility of the hierarchy between action and character in terms of the real reader, should be kept in mind. When s/he focuses on the action, this will be the center of attention, but whenever s/he focuses on the characters in the text, this aspect will dominate the reading process. Accordingly, the same procedure could be followed when these issues are addressed narratologically. I shall also follow this approach in this book.

For practical analysis of characters in Biblical narratives two issues are important, namely understanding the process of characterization and an ability to classify characters in a narrative text. These two issues will now be addressed.

The process of characterization

In order to understand the process of characterization, we can follow the procedures outlined by Seymour Chatman,[7] since it constitutes an easy, yet very accurate approach. It is based on the definition of characters in the narrative text in terms of *a paradigm of traits* - a trait being any relatively stable or abiding personal quality associated with a character. As such, the traits associated with a particular character may be unfolded, replaced or may even disappear in the course of the narrative. In practical terms this means that whenever an implied reader is confronted with a new character in the text, it opens a paradigm of traits to be associated with this particular character. As soon as it meets this character again in the text, it sorts through the paradigm of traits already associated with this character in order to account for any new information provided in terms of the traits already identified. If the new information cannot be accounted for in terms of these traits, a new trait will be added or a given trait will be reformulated, replaced or removed. Thus, if we want to analyze the process of characterization narratologically we have not only to reconstruct the paradigm of traits associated with each character, but we should also indicate the process whereby these traits are revealed by the implied author to the implied reader.

With regard to the process whereby traits are revealed to the implied reader, two processes are usually distinguished, namely direct and indirect characterization.[8]

Direct characterization

In the case of direct characterization a specific trait is mentioned directly, for example, by means of an adjective (He was a good man), an abstract noun (God is love) or another noun (She is a woman). However, what is important is to realize that the implied reader will always evaluate the specific trait mentioned in terms of other information in the text before adding it to the paradigm of traits. For example, an important issue in this regard is the question by whom the direct characterization is performed. If it is done by the narrator, it usually can be accepted. However, if it is performed by other characters in the text, direct characterization cannot always be accepted as trustworthy - especially not when it is performed by characters that are hostile to the character being characterized. Furthermore, issues such as the use of irony should also be kept in mind.

In Biblical narrative we have numerous examples of direct characterization. For example, in the Hebrew Bible Noah is described as "a righteous man, blameless in his generation" (Genesis 6:9), the people of Sodom as "wicked, great sinners against the Lord" (Genesis 13:13), Hannaniah as a "faithful man and feared God more than many" (Nehemiah 7:2) and Job as a man that was "blameless and upright, one who feared God and turned away from evil" (Job 1:1). In all these instances the implied author uses the narrator's voice to provide the direct characterization and accordingly it would be accepted by the implied reader as being correct. There are also examples of direct characterization performed by other voices in the text - all of which, after being evaluated by the implied reader, would be accepted or rejected. For example, Ester's direct characterization of Haman as "a foe and enemy, this wicked Haman!" (Esther 7:6) would be accepted by the implied reader as being correct in the light of the other information in the text, but Shimei's direct characterization of David as a "murderer and scoundrel" (2 Sam. 16:7) as not being correct.

In the Hebrew Bible we also have examples of direct characterization of a character that is to be re-evaluated by the implied reader in terms of additional evidence provided by the narrator. David Gunn and Danna Fewell[9] give an interesting example. In 2 Samuel 13:3 Ammon's friend and adviser, Jonadab, is characterized directly as a very wise man - a statement that has later to re-evaluated in terms of developments in the rest of this narrative.

In the New Testament quite a number of instances of direct characterization can be indicated, too. For example, Zechariah and Elizabeth are characterized as "righteous before God, living blamelessly according to all the commandments and regulations of God" (Luke 1:6), Simeon as "righteous and devout" (Luke 2:25), Tabitha as "devoted to good works and acts of charity" (Acts 9:36) and Stephen as "a man full of faith and the Holy Spirit" (Acts 6:5). In all of these instances the implied author uses the narrator to perform the direct characterization and therefore it will be accepted by the implied reader as being correct. In many instances direct characterization performed by other characters in the narrative world will, after evaluation, be accepted by the implied reader as being correct. For example, in the Gospel of Mark Jesus is characterized by Peter as the Christ (Mark 8:29) and by the centurion as the Son of God (Mark 15:39) - examples of direct characterization in line with the information received in the rest of the narrative. In some instances the implied reader will decide that the direct characterization is inadequate, ironically incorrect or outright wrong. The following examples will illustrate this: Nicodemus's direct characterization of Jesus as a teacher from God (John 3:2) is not wrong, but in terms of the other information provided by the implied author in the Gospel, it is clearly inadequate: according to this Gospel the best way to describe Jesus is to call him the Son of God. The Samaritan woman characterizes Jesus directly as someone who is surely not greater than their ancestor Jacob (John 4:12) - a characterization that is incorrect, but that is also heavily laden with irony. As an example of direct characterization that is outright wrong, John 8:48 can be cited where Jesus' opponents characterize him as a Samaritan who has a demon.

Indirect characterization

In the case of indirect characterization a given trait is not named, but portrayed or illustrated. The implied reader has to consider the information provided and formulate it in terms of a trait. The following may be used as means of indirect characterization:[10]

* A given trait may be illustrated by means of a character's *actions*. In this regard one should not only consider the actions actually performed by the character, but also those acts that could or should have been performed, but were not, as well as those acts that were only contemplated.

* A character's *speech* may also be used as a means of indirect characterization. Not only can the contents of a character's speech be indicative of certain traits, but also the style of speech may be indicative of a certain social class, profession or dwelling-place. In this regard irony can sometimes play a role.

* A character's external *appearance* may be handled in such a way that it

may serve as an indication of a given trait - not only those features partly dependent on the character him/herself (for example, clothing), but also those external features beyond a character's control (for example, physical appearance).

* The *environment* (physical surroundings) within which a character is portrayed, may be indicative of certain traits.

In the case of Biblical narratives it seems to me as if indirect characterization (especially the portrayal of actions of the characters) is by far the most popular way of informing the implied reader of certain traits of characters. From the overwhelming number of examples I shall only select a few to serve as illustration:

In the Hebrew Bible *actions* are used very often to illustrate certain traits. For example, in Genesis 12:1-4, the Lord's promise to Abram is narrated and then followed immediately by the words "So Abram went" - a deed that very clearly illustrates the trait of obedience to God. In many cases indirect characterization is used as the only means of characterization. For example, in the story of Cain (Gen 4:1-16) indirect characterization is used exclusively. Furthermore, deeds that could have been performed by characters but were not, are often used as important means of characterization, for example, the fact that Joseph refused to have sex with Potiphar's wife (Genesis 39:1-23) or Daniel's decision not to eat the royal rations of food and wine (Daniel 1:8).

Outward appearance is sometimes used in the Hebrew Bible as a means of indirect characterization, but usually does not play an important role. Sometimes characters are described as being beautiful, for example, Rachel (Gen. 29:17), Bathsheba (2 Sam. 11:2) and Tamar (2 Sam. 13:1). In itself beauty is not indicative of character as Meir Sternberg[11] points out in his excellent discussion of "three men with good looks" in the Book of Samuel: Saul, David and Absalom. The pattern that he detects in this regard is that the good looking man may crystallize either as good and successful or as bad and doomed, but (except in transitional phases) never as neither or both. In some instances we have indications of other external appearances in the Hebrew Bible, for example Esau's hairiness (Gen. 27:11), Ehud's left-handedness (Judges 3:15), Eglon's problem with overweight (Judges 3:17) and Goliath's height (1 Samuel 17:4) - all of which are not important as indicators of traits that these characters possess, but later play a significant role in the plot.

The use of *speech* as an indirect form of characterization of characters in the Hebrew Bible does not occur very often. Shimon Bar-Efrat[12] discusses the use of speech by characters in the Hebrew Bible at length and indicates that only a few examples can be found in this regard. For example, the disjointed sentences spoken by Ahimaaz in answer to David's question whether all was well with Absalom (2 Samuel 18:29) may reflect emotion, and Abigail's speech is distinguished by its figurative language (1 Samuel 25:24-31).

In the New Testament the portrayal of characters' *actions* is also used as a very important way of indirect characterization. Once again large numbers of examples could be cited, but I shall only mention a few: King Herod's deceitful nature is illustrated clearly in his dealings with the wise men (Matthew 2:1-12); the poor widow who throws the last two coins in her possession in the treasury thereby illustrates her devotion to God (Mark 12:41-44); and the rich young ruler's decision not to follow Jesus is illustrative of his love for his possessions (Luke 18:18-30). Furthermore, often characters' traits are revealed indirectly by actions that could have been performed, but were not. In some cases this is used to reveal or confirm negative traits possessed by the characters. For example, in the case of the disciples their inability to keep their promise to Jesus that they would follow him to the end, is perceived as an extremely negative action. In other cases an action not performed reveals or confirms traits that are considered to be positive by the implied author, for example, Peter and John's decision not to refrain from speaking about what they have seen and heard (Acts 4:19-20).

As in the case of the New Testament, *external appearance* is not used very often in characterization - even less so than in the Hebrew Bible - but a few instances can be indicated: John the Baptist's clothes of camel's hair and his leather belt are mentioned (Matthew 3:4) as well as Jesus' taking off of his outer robe in order to wash the disciples' feet (John 13:4). In some cases age is indicated: Jairus' daughter was twelve years old (Mark 5:42); Jesus was twelve years old when he stayed behind in the temple (Luke 2:42) and the man healed by Peter and John was over 40 years old (Acts 4:22).

Speech is not often used as a means of indirect characterization in the New Testament, but exceptions can be found as indicated in the case of the portrayal of Jesus in Luke. (See the discussion in chapter two, page 25.)

In the New Testament the *environment* within which characters are found, is often indicated. This may be used to reveal new traits to be associated by the character or it may have a supportive function in that it confirms information revealed in other ways. A few examples: John the Baptist lived in the desert (Mark 1:4); the prophet Anna was found constantly in the temple (Luke 2:37) and the man with an unclean spirit lived among the tombs (Mark 5:2).

In order to illustrate the way in which a paradigm of traits can be reconstructed for characters in Biblical narrative, I shall discuss two examples. There can be quite a difference in the number of traits associated with Biblical characters. This may vary from characters possessing a single trait to characters having quite a large number of traits.[13] In line with the scope of this book I shall discuss two examples in which only a relatively small paradigm of traits is associated with each character. In the case of characters with whom more extensive paradigms of traits are associated, the basic procedure will remain the same.

The first example is taken from the Hebrew Bible. The way in which a paradigm of traits can be reconstructed for the character *Ruth* will be discussed.

This character is introduced for the first time in Ruth 1:4 where the narrator is used by the implied author to reveal her name[14] and to characterize her directly as a Moabite. Accordingly, the first trait that will be listed by the implied reader in the paradigm of traits will be "foreigner" - a trait that will be repeated often in the rest of the narrative and plays a significant role. In the next verse the crisis that befell Naomi and Ruth is narrated. Although Naomi's desperate situation is emphasized in this verse, the implied reader will understand the disastrous consequences of Mahlon's death for Ruth, too: her social status was thereby changed to that of an impoverished widow. Accordingly this trait can also be added to the paradigm of traits.

In the next scene (1:6-18) another significant trait of this character is revealed, namely that of "self-sacrificing loyalty to Naomi". This is revealed by means of indirect characterization, especially by means of the contrast between Ruth and Orpah's behavior, namely that Ruth *clung*[15] to Naomi, as well as Ruth's remarkable words in 1:16-17.[16]

Another trait revealed by means of indirect characterization in this scene is Ruth's determination. This is seen in the way in which she pleaded with Naomi not to force her to leave, and is confirmed by the narrator in verse 18: "When Naomi saw that she was determined to go with her, she said no more to her." Ruth's actions in 2:2 where she is portrayed as taking the initiative by requesting Naomi to go to the field and glean among the ears of grain confirms this, too.[17]

In Ruth 2:3-16 (the first meeting between Ruth and Boaz) some of the traits revealed thus far are stressed again, for example, that she was a foreigner (by the narrator in 2:2, by the servant in 2:6 and by herself in 2:10); her desperate social position as an impoverished widow (by the servant in 2:6 and by her actions in 2:10); and her determination/ability to take initiative (by the servant in 2:7: "She has been on her feet from early in this morning until now, without resting even for a moment."). It is also revealed that Ruth was still young (see 2:5) - a fact that may have been gathered from the conversation between Naomi and Ruth in the first chapter, but is confirmed now for the first time. More important, however, is the way in which Ruth is characterized by Boaz: He calls her "my daughter" in 2:8 (expressing tenderness?[18]), cites the deeds showing her loyalty to Naomi (2:11),[19] and acts in such a way towards her that she can compare her position to that of his servants (2:13). Thus, although there is no definite indication at this stage that her social position will change, this possibility has at least been opened.

In the scene portrayed in 2:17-23 (Ruth's report to Naomi) no new traits are revealed, but some of those already known to the implied reader are repeated, for example, her loyalty to Naomi and the fact that she is a foreigner.

In Chapter three events take a significant turn. With regard to the characterization of Ruth two aspects are important: Firstly, Ruth's loyalty to Naomi (an important trait thus far) is demonstrated by her obedient reaction to Naomi's instructions. Secondly, in his reaction to Ruth's request to "spread his cloak over her", Boaz cites Ruth's good deeds (Ruth 3:10-13). The focal point of Boaz's reaction is his direct characterization of Ruth as a "worthy woman - as is known by all my people" (verse 11). This is a significant development. That Ruth is to be regarded as a "worthy woman" is already known to the implied reader (for example, this was clear from the loyal way in which she treated Naomi), but the fact that one of the important characters in the narrative, who is in a position to change Ruth's desperate social situation, acknowledges this, is important. In fact, by having Boaz attest to Ruth's worthiness, the implied author suggests to the implied reader that Ruth deserved a social position equal to that of Boaz -

whom the narrator characterized earlier on (2:1) as a "man of substance" - very similar to "worthy woman".[20]

In the last chapter Ruth's social position is changed. In 4:5 Boaz characterizes her directly as "Ruth, the Moabite, the widow of the dead man" in his dealings with the kinsman (4:5). This is repeated in more or less the same words in his legal dealings in the presence of the witnesses at the city gate (4:10) - after which Ruth's social status is changed to that of Boaz's wife. In this way Ruth's progress from "impoverished widow" via "worthy woman" reaches its logical end as "wife of a man of substance". But there is more to come: In the last four verses the implied author uses the narrator to recount a genealogy, beginning with Perez and ending with king David. In terms of the characterization of Ruth, a last significant trait is revealed to the implied reader, namely that she was an ancestress of king David!

In order to conclude this discussion of the characterization of Ruth, the following paradigm of traits can be reconstructed (the arrows indicate development or new phases of characterization)

Ruth: Paradigm of traits

* Socially: foreigner
* Self-sacrificing loyalty (to Naomi)
* Socially: impoverished widow » worthy woman » wife of a man of substance
* Determination/ability to take initiative
* Relatively young
* Ancestress of king David

As an example of characterization in the New Testament I shall discuss Judas Iscariot. Although this character can be classified as one of the minor figures in the New Testament, he is nevertheless one of the most fascinating figures in it. Since he is mentioned in all four Gospels, I shall also indicate how the paradigm of traits associated with him differs from Gospel to Gospel.[21]

In the Gospel of Mark, Judas is portrayed as a character possessing only a single trait. In other words: the paradigm of traits associated with this character contains only one trait. In Mark 3:14-19 the implied author introduces him for the first time when the narrator is used to recount the list of the twelve disciples. Judas is mentioned last and is characterized directly as the one who betrayed Jesus. Accordingly the implied reader will associate the trait of treacherousness with this character. A second reference to Judas is found in Mark 14:10-11 where the narrator recounts that Judas went to the chief priests in order to betray Jesus. This act (thus indirect characterization) is in line with the trait already identified in Mark 3:14-19. It is important to note that the implied reader does not make any attempt to provide a psychological motivation that would explain Judas's behavior. In verse 11 the narrator tells that the chief priests promised to give him money, but this is worded in such a way that it does not seem as if this was the driving force behind Judas's action. In Mark 14:18-21 the implied reader meets Judas again - although he is not mentioned explicitly. The narrator tells how Jesus informed the disciples that one of them would betray him. Distressed, the disciples "one after another" says to him: "Surely, not I?" The implied reader will assume that Judas reacted in the same way - an act that indirectly characterizes him again as treacherous. In Mark 14:43-45 Judas is mentioned for the last time: He appears with a crowd of people, goes to Jesus, calls him "Rabbi" and identifies him with a kiss. Once again his actions are used to characterize him indirectly as treacherous. Thus, in the Gospel of Mark Judas is characterized as a figure having this trait only.

In the Gospel of Matthew Judas is mentioned five times: Matthew 10:1-4; 26:14-16; 26:20-25; 26:47-50; 27:3-10. Once again, the trait of treacherousness is indicated as the primary trait. However, in comparison with the Gospel of Mark the paradigm of traits is slightly larger:

* Treacherousness
* Avarice
* Ability to repent/have remorse

The first trait is portrayed in the first four passages and, as I have indicated, it is the most important trait of the three. The second trait is illustrated by means of indirect characterization in Matthew 26:14-16: Judas goes to the chief priests and asks them: "What will you give me if I betray him to you?" (Note the difference from Mark's version!) Judas thus takes the initiative and is clearly interested in the possibility of financial gain - a fact from which the implied reader can deduce the trait of avarice. Furthermore, in this way Judas's decision to betray Jesus is motivated psychologically. The third trait is portrayed in Matt. 27:3-10: Judas realizes that Jesus is innocent, repents, takes back the thirty silver pieces to the chief priests and in the end hangs himself - thereby illustrating his ability to have remorse.

In Luke-Acts Judas is mentioned five times: Luke 6:13-16; 22:3-6; 22:21-23 (implicitly); 22:47-48 and Acts 1:15-20. The paradigm of traits associated with Judas in Luke-Acts consists of only two traits:

* Treacherousness
* Inspired by Satan

The first trait is conveyed by means of either direct or indirect characterization in all the passages. The second trait is introduced in Luke 22:3-6 where the narrator explains Judas's decision to go to the chief priests as follows: "Then Satan entered Judas ...". In line with the emphasis placed on this aspect, the implied author does not motivate Judas's decision explicitly in terms of avarice. In verse 5 a sum of money is mentioned, but it is linked to the initiative of the chief priests. It is also important to note that, although Judas's end is recounted in Acts 1:15-20, there is no sign of remorse. Indeed it happens in a totally different way from Matthew's version: Judas bought a piece of land and then "falling headlong, he burst open in the middle and all his bowls gushed out". The absence of the trait "ability to repent/show remorse" can be explained in terms of the new trait introduced by the implied author in Luke-Acts, namely that Judas was inspired by Satan.

In the Gospel of John Judas is mentioned five times: John 6:70-71; 12:1-8; 13:1-30; 17:12b and 18:1-11. The paradigm of traits associated with Judas in the Gospel of John can be summarized as follows:

* Treacherousness
* Inspired by Satan
* Thief
* Son of perdition

The first trait is the dominant one and is illustrated in all the passages. The other three traits serve as an explanation for Judas's actions. The second trait is emphasized three times: In John 6:70 Jesus calls the traitor a devil; in John 13:2 the narrator links Judas's decision to betray Jesus directly to Satan who "had already put it into his heart"; and in John 13:30 the narrator dramatically recounts that Satan entered Judas exactly at the moment when he took the piece of bread from Jesus. The third trait (that Judas was also a thief) is revealed in the scene in John 12:1-8 in which Jesus is anointed by Mary. In verse 6 Judas is characterized directly by the narrator as a thief and this is explained as follows: "He kept the common purse and used to steal what was put into it". The fourth trait - that Judas was the "son of perdition" is revealed in Jesus' Prayer of Farewell in John 17:12b. "Son of perdition" is an indication that Judas was inspired by the Satan, but there is more to it. It refers to the one who belongs to the realm of damnation and is destined for final destruction. Furthermore, it may also be used to refer to the Antichrist (see 2 Thessalonians 2:3) - an indication that Judas may be characterized in John 17:12b as a manifestation of the Antichrist.[22]

Classification of characters

In the analysis of characters in Biblical texts it can be helpful to use existing systems for the classification of characters. Quite a number of these systems have been developed by literary critics, but I shall only discuss four.

E. M. Forster

The oldest of the four systems discussed here, is the one developed by E. M. Forster.[23] He distinguishes between so-called "flat" and "round" characters. "Flat" characters are described as caricatures or types that embody only a single idea or quality (trait). Furthermore they do not show any development in the course of the discourse. "Round characters" are complex characters who have more than one quality (trait) and who show signs of development during the course of action. In order to have a criterion for deciding whether a character should be classified as round or flat, Forster suggests that a character who is capable of surprising the reader in a convincing way, should be classified as a round character.

Forster's distinction between flat and round characters have been used often - also by Biblical scholars, but a warning note should be sounded in this regard. Although the distinction can be helpful, it suffers from several weaknesses. For example, the distinction (especially the criterion cited above) is formulated so vaguely that it really is very difficult to apply it fruitfully to Biblical texts. Furthermore, the distinction between "flat" and "round" can imply a moral judgement of the characters in the sense that round characters are usually considered as being superior to flat characters.[24]

The best way to use Forster's distinction seems to be to distinguish between flat and round characters primarily in terms of the number of traits associated with each character and/or whether there is any development. See, for instance, the way in which Ferdinand Deist[25], applies the distinction between flat and round characters to the different ways in which David is portrayed in Chronicles and Samuel-Kings:

> When, for instance, the David character in the Samuel-Kings narrative is compared with the David character in Chronicles, the distinction is readily apparent. In Samuel-Kings, David is confronted with many problematic decisions; he has to face relatives, subjects, equals and superiors, friends and foes; he appears as a brigand, a diplomat, a king, a father, a husband, and so

forth. Now he is sympathizing with an enemy on the death of his father, then he murders one of his subjects in order to have his wife for himself; now he deals ruthlessly with his enemies, then he flees before his son Absalom. The David character in Chronicles, however, is a stereotype - not a fallible human being but a faultless priest and a founder of the cult. The David of the Books of Chronicles is purely and simply an 'argument' for the validity of the temple rites in Jerusalem - an abstract justification of an existing institution. The character of David in Samuel-King develops (by degeneration), but the David of Chronicles *is* as he is - like a philosophy or static idea.

Another alternative is to replace Forster's classification by another classification that could be used with better results. For example, Adele Berlin[26] replaces his classification with a three-fold classification thereby providing a better framework for classifying characters in the narratives in the Hebrew Bible. These are the following:

Full-fledged characters (corresponding to Forster's round characters): characters that are complex, manifesting a multitude of traits, and appearing as "real people".
Types (corresponding to Forster's flat characters): characters that are built around a single trait or quality.
Agents: characters that serve as mere functionaries and are not characterized at all.

W. J. Harvey

Harvey[27] uses the following three categories for classifying characters: The important characters in the narrative are called the *protagonists*. They are characterized more fully than the others, are more complex and change as the narrative progresses. On the other end of the scale we have the so-called *background characters* who are not characterized extensively and whose only function is to serve as a part of the mechanics of the plot. In between the protagonists and the background characters we have a third category of intermediary figures of which two types are distinguished: A *card* is a character who approaches greatness, but who is not cast into the role of a protagonist. It is relatively changeless, and may be comic and pathetic at the same time. The second type of intermediary character Harvey calls *ficelles*. These are usually characterized more extensively than the background characters, yet exist only with the purpose of fulfilling certain functions within the narrative, for example, as transitional agents between the protagonist and society, as foils to the protagonist, or as alternative to the protagonist.

Joseph Ewen

Ewen[28] proposes that characters should be viewed in terms of points along a continuum and not be classified in terms of exhaustive categories. He distinguishes the following three axes on which the way in which each character is characterized can be located:

* Complexity: A continuum that varies from those characters displaying a single trait to those displaying a complex paradigm of traits.

* Development: A continuum that varies from those characters that show no development at all to those who undergo an intensive development in the narrative.

* Penetration into inner life: A continuum that varies from those characters who are viewed ("focalized") continually from the outside to those characters whose inner life is portrayed extensively.

A. J. Greimas

J. Greimas[29] who is a well-known figure within Structuralism has developed the following actantial model, according to which all the characters in a narrative text can be reduced to six actants, that is general categories underlying all narrative texts - even if this implies that the same actant is manifested in more than one character, or that more than one character should be reduced to the same actant:

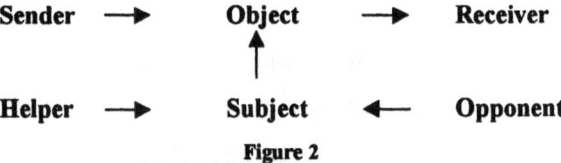

Figure 2

These actants can be defined as follows:[30]

* The object is the goal or destination of the action.
* The subject is the performative agency of the action.
* The sender initiates or enables the event.
* The receiver benefits from or registers the effect of the event.
* The opponent retards or impedes the event by opposing the subject or by competing with the subject for the object.
* The helper advances or fulfills the action by supporting or assisting the subject.

In order to illustrate the way in which the classification of characters can be performed in Biblical narrative, I shall discuss one example. In John 13:1-17:26 the following events on the evening before Jesus' crucifixion are narrated: The Footwashing, the identification of Judas as the traitor, the announcement of Jesus' departure, the announcement of Peter's denial, a number of farewell discourses and a prayer of farewell. The following characters form part of the narrated world in John 13:1-17:26: God (usually called "Father"), Jesus, the Holy Spirit ("Paraclete"), the disciples as a group and as individuals (Peter, Judas Iscariot, Thomas, Philip and Judas), the world and Satan.[31] If these characters are classified in terms of the four systems discussed above, the following emerges:

The weakness of the system of *E. M. Forster* can be illustrated very effectively in this case. If the criterion indicated by Forster himself is used, namely whether a character is capable of surprising the implied reader in a convincing way, none of the characters (not even Jesus) can be classified as round figures, since nothing that any of the characters does, will really surprise the implied reader. As I have suggested above, a better criterion for deciding whether a character is round or flat would be to distinguish between them on account of the number of traits associated with each character. (See the aspect of "complexity" in Ewen's system below.)

If the classification of *Harvey* is used, Jesus should be classified as the protagonist. All the other characters are to be classified as ficelles, since they are all portrayed primarily in terms of their relationship to Jesus.

If Ewen's classification is used, the characters should be classified as follows:

	Complexity	Development	Penetration
Jesus	Very complex	None	A little
The Father	Complex	None	None
Paraclete	Complex	None	None
Disciples	Not complex	None	A little
World	Not complex	None	None
Peter	Not complex	None	None
Judas Iscariot	Single trait	None	None
Thomas	Single trait	None	None
Philip	Single trait	None	None
Judas	Single trait	None	None

If *Greimas's* actantial system is used, we can discern two models:

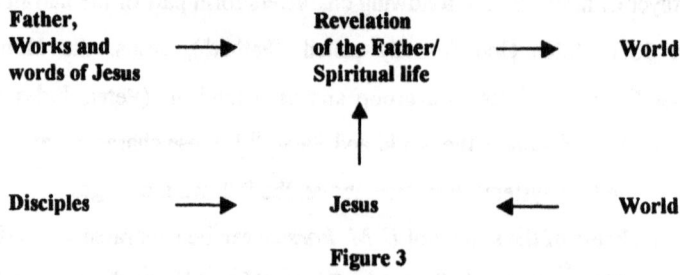

Figure 3

In the first model (figure 3) Jesus is the subject who pursues the object of revealing the Father and providing spiritual life to the "world" (receiver). The words and works of Jesus, as well as the Father himself, are classified as the sender, since they enable the subject to pursue the object. The disciples are the helpers and the "world" is classified as the opponent. The first model indicates the situation on the evening before the crucifixion.

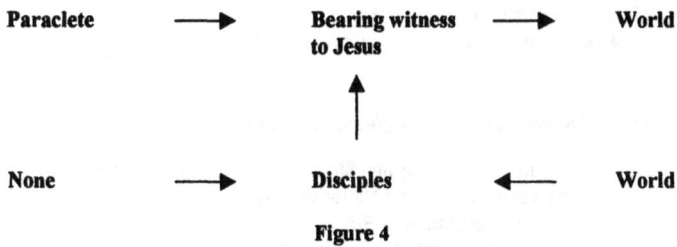

Figure 4

The second model (figure 4) indicates the future situation as foretold by Jesus (on that evening). The disciples will be (should be) the subject pursuing the object of witnessing to the "world" (the receiver). The Paraclete (and Jesus through the Paraclete) will enable the disciples to reach the object and is therefore classified as the helper. The "world" is also classified as the opponent, since it will try to prevent the subject from reaching the object.

In the case of John 13:1-17:26 it seems as if the models of Ewen and Greimas can be used with the most success. However, this cannot be accepted as a general rule and one has to decide this matter from narrative to narrative.

Suggestions for further reading on the theoretical issues of analyzing characters

Bal, Mieke. *Narratology. Introduction to the Theory of Narrative.* Toronto: University of Toronto Press, 1985: 25-36; 79-91.
Chatman, Seymour. "On the Formalist-Structuralist Theory of Character", *Journal of Literary Semantics* 1 (1972): 57-79.
Chatman, Seymour. *Story and Discourse.* London: Ithaca, 1978: 108-133.
Cixous, Helene. "The Character of 'Character'", *New Literary History* 5 (1974): 383-402.
Cohan, Steven & Shires, Linda M. *Telling Stories. A Theoretical Analysis of Narrative Fiction.* New York: Routledge, 1988: 72-76.
Crittenden, Charles. "Fictional Characters and Logical Completeness", *Poetics* 11 (1982): 331-344.
Forster, E. M. *Aspects of the Novel.* London: Edward Arnold, 1944.
Garvey, James. "Characterisation in Narrative", *Poetics* 7 (1978): 63-78.
Harvey, W. J. *Character and the Novel.* London: Chatto & Windus, 1965.
Hochman, Baruch. *Character in Literature.* Ithaca: Cornell, 1985.
Kenney, William. *How to Analyse Fiction.* New York: Monard, 1966: 24-37.
Martin, Wallace. *Recent Theories of Narrative.* Ithaca: Cornell, 1986: 116-122.
Mudrick, Marvin. "Characters and Event in Fiction", *YR* 59 (1961): 202-218.

Phelan, James. *Reading People, Reading Plots. Character, Progression, and the Interpretation of Narrative.* Chicago: University of Chicago Press, 1989.
Prince, Gerald. *A Dictionary of Narratology.* University of Nebraska Press, 1987.

Suggestions for further reading on characterization in Biblical narrative

Bar-Efrat, Shimon. *Narrative Art in the Bible.* Sheffield: Almond, 1989: 47-92.
Berlin, Adele. "Characterization in Biblical Narrative: David's Wives", *JSOT* 23 (1982): 69-85.
Berlin, Adele. *Poetics and Interpretation of Biblical Narrative.* Sheffield: Almond, 1983: 23-40.
Black, C. Clifton III. "Dept of Characterisation and Degrees of Faith in Matthew", in *1989 SBL Seminar Papers,* ed. David J. Lull, (Atlanta: Scholars Press, 1989), 604-623.
Brenner, Athalya. "Job the Pious? The Character of Job in the Narrative Framework of the Book", *JSOT* 43 (1989): 37-52.
Culpepper, R. Alan. *Anatomy of the Fourth Gospel. A Study in Literary Design.* Philadelphia: Fortress, 1983: 99-148.
Danove, Paul. "The Characterization and Narrative Function of the Women at the Tomb (Mark 15,40-41.47; 16,1-8)", *Bib* 77/3 (1996): 375-397.
Darr, John A. *Paradigms of Perception: The Reader and the Characters of Luke-Acts.* Louisville: Westminster, 1992.
Day, Linda. *Three Faces of a Queen. Characterization in the Books of Esther.* Sheffield: Sheffield Academic Press, 1995.
Gowler, David B. *Host, Guest, Enemy and Friend: Portraits of the Pharisees in Luke and Acts.* New York: Peter Lang, 1991.
Green, Barbara. "The Determination of Pharaoh: His Characterization in the Joseph Story (Genesis 37-50), in *The World of Genesis. Persons, Places, Perspectives,* eds. Philip R. Davies & David J. A. Clines (Sheffield: Sheffield Academic Press, 1998), 150-171.
Gunn, David & Fewell, Danna Nolan. *Narrative in the Hebrew Bible.* Oxford: Oxford University Press, 1993: 46-89.
Jeansonne, Sharon Pace. "The Character of Lot in Genesis", *BTB* 18 (1988): 123-129.
Kingsbury, Jack Dean. "The Figure of Jesus in Matthew's Story: A Literary-Critical Probe", *JSNT* 21 (1984): 3-36.
Kisling, Paul J. *Reliable Characters in the Primary History. Profiles of Moses, Joshua, Elijah and Elisha.* Sheffield: Sheffield Academic Press, 1996.
Klauck, Hans-Josef. "Die erzählerische Rolle der Jünger im Markusevangelium. Eine narrative Analyse", *NT* 24/1 (1982): 1-26.
Malbon, Elizabeth Struthers & Berlin, Adele. Eds. Characterization in Biblical Literature. *Semeia* 63 (1993).
Malbon, Elizabeth Struthers. "Disciples/Crowds/Whoever: Markan Characters and Readers", *NT* 28 (1986): 104-130.
Malbon, Elizabeth Struthers. "The Major Importance of Minor Characters in Mark", in *The New Literary Criticism and the New Testament,* eds. Elizabeth Struthers Malbon & Edgar V. Knight, (Sheffield: Sheffield Academic Press, 1994), 58-86.
Noll, K.L. *The Faces of David.* Sheffield: Sheffield Academic Press, 1997.
O'Brien, Mark A. "The Contribution of Judah's Speech, Genesis 44:18-34, to the Characterization of Joseph", *CBQ* 59/3 (1997): 429-447.
Perdue, Leo. G. "Is There Anyone Left in the House of Saul...? Ambiguity and the Characterization of David in the Succession Narrative", *JSOT* 30 (1984): 67-84.
Person, Raymond F. *In Conversation with Jonah: Conversation Analysis, Literary Criticism and the Book of Jonah.* Sheffield: Sheffield Academic Press, 1996: 54-67.

Powell, Mark Allan. "The Religious Leaders in the Gospel of Luke: A Literary-Critical Study", *JBL* 109 (1990): 103-120.

Roth, S. John. *The Blind, the Lame and the Poor. Character Types in Luke-Acts*. Sheffield: Sheffield Academic Press, 1997.

Shepherd, William H. *The Narrative Function of the Holy Spirit in Luke-Acts*. Atlanta: Scholars Press, 1994.

Smartley, Willard M. "The Role of Women in Mark's Gospel: A Narrative Analysis", *BTB* 27/1 (1997): 16-22.

Staley, Jeffrey L. "Stumbling in the Dark, Reaching for the Light: Reading Character in John 5 and 9", *Semeia* 53 (1991): 55-80.

Sternberg, Meir. *The Poetics of Biblical Narrative. Ideological Literature and the Drama of Reading*. Bloomington: Indiana University Press, 1985: 321-364.

Thiemann, Ronald F. "The Unnamed Woman at Bethany", *ThTo* 44 (1987): 179-188.

Tolmie, D. Francois. "The Characterization of God in the Fourth Gospel", *JSNT* 69 (1998): 57-75.

Vorster, Willem S. "Characterization of Peter in the Gospel of Mark", *Neotest* 21 (1987): 57-76.

Walsh, Jerome T. "The Characterization of Solomon in First Kings 1-5", *CBQ* 57 (1995): 471-493.

Notes

[1] See Rimmon-Kenan, *Narrative Fiction*, 31-36, for a detailed discussion of what follows.

[2] See Marvin Mudrick, "Character and Event in Fiction", *YR* 50 (1961): 202-218.

[3] Formalism is a tendency in Theory of Literature according to which the meaning of a text is located in the details of its structure, whereas those who follow Structuralism attempt to analyze texts in terms of transhistorical and transcultural generative systems on which they believe production of meaning is based. See Stephen D. Moore, *Literary Criticism*, 181-183.

[4] *Morphology of the Folktale* (Austin: Texas, 1968).

[5] "Theory and Model for the Structural Analysis of Fiction", *New Literary History* 5 (1974): 245-268.

[6] *Narrative Fiction*, 35-36.

[7] *Story and Discourse*, 119-133.

[8] For the following see Rimmon-Kenan, *Narrative Fiction*, 59-67.

[9] *Narrative in the Hebrew Bible*, 61-62.

[10] Rimmon-Kenan, *Narrative Fiction*, 59-67.

[11] *The Poetics of Biblical Narrative*, 354-362.

[12] *Narrative Art in the Bible*, 64-69.

[13] For example, the paradigm of traits associated with Jesus in the Fourth Gospel consists of more than 40 traits! See my *Jesus' Farewell to the Disciples. John 13:1-17:26 in Narratological Perspective* (Leiden: E. J. Brill, 1995), 125-126.

[14] Since it is not clear whether the name Ruth should be interpreted as "woman companion" or "friend", I shall not add this to the paradigm of traits. See Edward J. Campbell, *Ruth. A New Translation with Introduction, Notes and Commentary* (New York: Doubleday, 1975), 57.

[15] The Hebrew expression implies absolute loyalty and even erotic affection. See Robert L. Hubbard, *The Book of Ruth* (Grand Rapids: Eerdmans, 1988), 115.

[16] Danna Nolan Fewell & David Miller Gunn, *Compromising Redemption. Relating Characters in the Book of Ruth* (Louisville: Westminster, John Knox, 1990), 97-98, suggest that Ruth's behavior may have been motivated primarily by a desire to look out for herself, and not by an attitude of radical self-sacrifice. However, it seems to me as if the way in which the implied author contrasts

the behavior of Ruth and Orpah, should incline one to prefer the interpretation provided in my analysis. Also see Phyllis Trible, *God and the Rhetoric of Sexuality* (Philadelphia: Fortress, 1978), 173, who emphasizes the radicalness of Ruth's decision.

[17] See, Ramona Faye West, *Ruth: A Retelling of Genesis 38?* (Ann Arbor: University Microfilms International, 1987), 116-117.

[18] See Hubbard, *Ruth*, 154.

[19] Robert Alter, *The World of Biblical Literature* (New York: Basic Books, 1992), 51-52, draws attention to the correspondence between the way in which Boaz's words are phrased in this scene and God's words to Abraham in Genesis 12:1, and proposes an interesting thesis, namely that Ruth is set up as a founding mother, in symmetrical correspondence to the founding father, Abraham.

[20] The same Hebrew word is used in 2:1 and 3:11. See Edward F. Campbell, *Ruth*, 124-125.

[21] For a more detailed discussion of the portrayal of Judas in the Bible and in Western imagination, see Hyam Maccoby, *Judas Iscariot and the Myth of Jewish Evil* (New York: Free Press, 1992).

[22] This is in line with the emphasis on realized eschatology in the Gospel of John and the Johannine Letters. See Raymond E. Brown, *The Gospel According to John. Volume 2: John 13-21* (London: Geoffrey Chapman, 1966), 760.

[23] *Aspects of the Novel* (London: Edward Arnold, 1944), 93-106.

[24] K. D. Beekman & J. Fontijn, "Roman-figuren I", *Spektator* 1 (1971): 406-413.

[25] *Words from Afar: The Literature of the Old Testament. Volume 1* (Cape Town: Tafelberg, 1989), 98-99.

[26] *Poetics*, 23-24.

[27] *Character and the Novel* (London: Chatto & Windus, 1965).

[28] Ewen's study "The Theory of Character in Narrative Fiction", *Hasifrut* 3 (1974): 1-30, is unfortunately only available in Hebrew. See Rimmon-Kenan, *Narrative Fiction*, 40-42, for a discussion.

[29] *Sémantique structurale. Recherche dé méthode* (Paris: Librairie Larousse, 1966), 172-191.

[30] See Cohan & Shires, *Telling Stories*, 69.

[31] See my *Jesus' Farewell to the Disciples. John 13:1-17:26 in Narratological Perspective* (Leiden: Brill, 1995), 117-143, for a detailed discussion of what follows.

CHAPTER FIVE

EVENTS

Defining an event is not very difficult. One could say that anything that happens to someone/something or anything that is done by something/something is an event. If a more formal definition is required, the one provided by Steven Cohan and Linda M. Shires[1] seems to be right on target:

> An *event* depicts some sort of physical or mental activity, an occurrence in time (an action performed by or upon a human agent) or a state of existing in time (such as thinking, feeling, being or having).

Whenever we read a narrative, we are confronted with a number of events that are organized and presented to us in a certain way. This "interpretative ordering of events"[2] - usually called the *plot* of the narrative - is the important issue to be addressed in this chapter. In this chapter I shall discuss some of the procedures that may be followed in order to analyze events and the combination of events in individual narratives.

The procedures outlined in this chapter are based on the assumption that the organization of events in narrative texts can be analyzed from two different, yet complementary perspectives. On the one hand, the events in the narrative text are organized syntagmatically, that is, they are narrated one after the other. This can be called the *surface structure* of events. On the other hand, it is also possible to analyze the events in the narrative text in terms of a paradigmatic structure. In other words, the various events may also be analyzed in terms of the ways in which they are related to one another, for example, in terms of the oppositions that can be detected between groups of events. These relationships are not necessarily indicated on the surface level, but can be inferred in terms of the underlying logic in the text. This aspect is called the *deep structure* of events.[3]

I shall discuss procedures for the analysis of the *surface structure* first.

The surface structure of events

The procedure for analyzing the surface structure of events can be divided into three steps:[4]

    a) Paraphrasing the events
    b) Classifying the events
    c) Determining the relationship between the events

The *paraphrasing of events* can be achieved in various ways, but the most useful option seems to be to paraphrase each event in terms of a single sentence in such a way that the subject performing the action, as well as the action that is being performed, is clearly indicated, for example: Peter kicks the ball.

The next step is devoted to the *classification of the events* and is followed in order to distinguish between the various types of events (as paraphrased in the previous step). In this regard there are various systems that may be used. One of these is the one used by Seymour Chatman,[5] which can be summarized as follows: As a first distinction, *actions* and *happenings* can be distinguished. Although both are changes of state, in the case of actions a character is the narrative subject (not necessarily the grammatical subject) of the event. Example: The thief stole the diamonds/the diamonds were stolen by the thief. In the case of happenings, a character is the narrative object of the event. Example: The storm casts Peter adrift.

The first category distinguished, *actions*, may be classified further in terms of the following five principal kinds of actions:[6]

> *External events*
> 1 Verbal acts (He told me to leave.)
> 2 Non-verbal physical acts (He pushed me out of the door.)
> *Internal events*
> 3 Mental acts (I thought about leaving.)
> 4 Emotional events (I felt uneasy about leaving.)
> 5 Sensory events (I heard someone leaving.)

A further distinction that may be useful is the distinction between *durative events* (for example, she loves him) and *punctual events* (for example, he kicks his dog). I would suggest that the distinctions outlined above should not be regarded as a rigid system for classifying events, but only as a general guideline indicating how it can be achieved. In the end one should classify the events in the specific narrative text in such a way that it can be used for further interpretation, and therefore the system used should suit this purpose. For example, in the case of a narrative consisting of more than 90% verbal acts, the system outlined above will not be of great use. In such a case it would be better to use another system such as speech act theory, since it may produce much better results.[7]

The last issue to be discussed is the procedure for *determining the relationships between events*. In this regard two important aspects should be considered.

First of all the *hierarchy* between events must be considered. Some events are more important that others. Accordingly, one can distinguish between those events that are crucial to the logic of the plot and others that may be deleted without disturbing the logic of the plot (although their omission will impoverish the narrative in other ways). The events that are absolutely crucial to the understanding of the logic of the plot are called *kernels* by Seymour Chatman[8] whereas the other events are called *satellites*. These are defined as follows:

> Kernels are narrative moments that give rise to cruxes in the direction taken by events. They are nodes or hinges in the structure, branching points which force a movement into one of two (or more) possible paths ... Satellites entail no choice, but are solely the workings-out of the choices made at the kernels. They necessarily imply the existence of kernels, but not vice versa. Their function is that of filling in, elaborating, completing the kernel; they form the flesh on the skeleton.[9]

The second procedure is to combine the individual events into *microsequences*, which, in turn, should be combined into *macrosequences*. In this regard the distinctions between kernels and satellites could be helpful, but this is not always the case. Accordingly, the indication of microsequences can be rather subjective. The best approach seems to be to combine the events that fit logically together. For example, consider the following series of events:

1 John picked up his gun.
2 John aimed at Peter.
3 John pulled the trigger.
4 The bullet hit Peter in his temple.
5 Peter fell on the ground.
6 Peter started bleeding.
7 Peter died

These seven events can be regarded as a microsequence and summarized as "John killed Peter". In the same way, a number of microsequences can be combined to form one macrosequence, which, in turn, can be combined with other macrosequences to form a series of macrosequences.

However, it is not enough to merely indicate the groups of micro- and macrosequences of events. It is also necessary to ask the question whether the implied author has provided any clues with regard to the way in which the micro/macrosequences are combined. The principles used in the combination of micro/macrosequences are important as they provide a basis for describing the interpretative ordering of events - an aspect which usually is vital to understanding the ideological perspective of a narrative.

As to the various principles that may be used for combining micro/macrosequences, the following five can be pointed out:[10]

* *Time*: The implied reader will usually assume that, unless indications are given to the contrary, events are narrated in a chronological order. (For a detailed discussion of the various ways in which the temporal aspect of narrative texts can be manipulated, see the following chapter.)

* *Causality*: One micro/macrosequence may serve as the cause of another micro/macrosequence.

* *Space*: Micro/macrosequences may also be combined by the fact that they are situated in the same geographical location.

* *Character*: Micro/macrosequences may be dominated by the same character(s). In such a case the principle of character can be indicated.

* *Internal relationships*: In some cases structural relationships can be indicated between various groups of micro-/macrosequences. In this regard issues such as contrast and similarity, as well as stylistic issues (for example, the use of chiasms) should be considered.

The deep structure of events

In order to study the deep structure of events we have to try to uncover the paradigmatic relations between events. Unfortunately this is a more complicated process, since we have to uncover the *underlying logic* of the narrative - something that is not necessarily mentioned explicitly in the surface structure. There are various ways to go about determining and representing the deep structure of events, but, following Rimmon-Kenan,[11] I would suggest the use of the semiotic square developed by Greimas. The semiotic square forms part of a comprehensive semiotic theory, called the generative trajectory[12] where it is used to describe various semantic levels.

Greimas's semiotic theory is very complicated, but for our purpose it will suffice to know that a semiotic square may be used as a visual representation of the underlying logic of the narrative text. In order to determine the underlying logical relations in a narrative text, one should try to isolate lines of meaning or isotopies in the text.[13] An isotopy is defined by David Jobling[14] as follows:

> A semantic category defined broadly enough to subsume a large number of elements of meaning in the text, but precisely enough for useful organization of these elements.

In order to determine isotopies, it is useful to look for groupings of events that are portrayed as or imply opposing categories. Examples of these are the following:[15]

* Opposing types of events (good/bad; love/hate)
* Opposing locations (inside/outside)
* Opposing groups of characters (friends/enemies)

Once the most important isotopies have been distinguished, the contents of each isotopy have to be analyzed in terms of its logical relations. Greimas distinguishes three types of relations that may exist:[16]

* Contradictory: If it becomes clear that the contents of the isotopy do not only differ, but are also mutually exclusive, the relationship can be described as contradictory. Examples: white and ~~white~~; poor and ~~poor~~. (The strikethrough characters indicate a negation: not white, not poor.) When textual elements are regarded as contradictory, these elements indicate extremes between which no intermediate position/value is possible.

* Contrary: If the contents of the isotopy are different from each other, yet mutually inclusive, the relationship between them is regarded as contrary. Accordingly they are presented in the text as opposites, but each presupposes the existence of the other. Example: poor and rich. When textual elements are regarded as being contrary, the elements indicate extremes between which intermediate positions/values are possible, for example grey (between black and white).

* Complementary: If the elements distinguished in the isotopy are related to each other in such a way that the absence of one is a condition for the presence of the other element, the relationship is regarded as being complementary. Examples ~~rich~~ implies poor and ~~poor~~ implies rich.

These relationships can be presented in terms of a semiotic square:

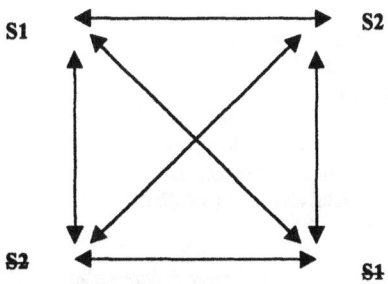

Figure 5

* S1/S2 and ~~S2/S1~~: Contrary relationship
* S1/~~S1~~ and S2/~~S2~~: Contradictory relationship
* S1/~~S2~~ and S2/~~S1~~: Complementary relationships

It should also be noted that the semiotic square could also be used to indicate the dynamics of the underlying logical structure. This can be indicated by means of arrows in the semiotic square. For example, if the plot or a part of it is devoted to the marriage of a bachelor, the following movement can be indicated on the semiotic square:

Bachelor (S1) » ~~bachelor~~ (~~S1~~) » married man (S2).[17]

In order to illustrate the way in which events can be analyzed in a narratological analysis, I shall discuss two examples.

The first example comes from the Hebrew Bible: Gen. 2:4b-3:25.[18] I shall first discuss the organization of the surface structure. In the following diagram you will find the result of the following procedures:

a) A paraphrasing of all the events
b) A classification of all the events
c) An indication of the kernels (underlined)
d) A summary of micro-sequences (italics)

A: *God creates man.*
1 God forms man from the dust. — Physical act
2 God breathes into his nostrils to make him a human being — Physical act

B: *God creates a garden in Eden.*
1 <u>God plants a garden in Eden.</u> — Physical act
2 <u>God places man in the garden.</u> — Physical act
3 God makes many trees grow in the garden: pleasant for sight and good for good — Physical act
4 <u>God places the tree of life and the tree of knowledge of good and evil in the garden.</u> — Physical act
5 A river flows out of Eden. — Physical act

C: *God forbids man to eat of the tree of knowledge of good and evil.*
1 God places man in the garden to till and keep it. — Physical act
2 <u>God forbids man to eat of the tree of knowledge of good and evil.</u> — Verbal act: Prohibition

D: *God creates woman.*
1 <u>God decides to create a partner for man.</u> — Mental act
2 God creates animals and birds. — Physical act
3 God brings them to man. — Physical act
4 Man gives names to all creatures. — Verbal act: Naming
5 Man looks in vain for a partner. — Physical act
6 God causes a deep sleep to fall upon man. — Physical act
7 God takes one of man's ribs. — Physical act
8 God closes the place with flesh. — Physical act
9 <u>God creates woman.</u> — Physical act
10 God brings her to man. — Physical act
11 Man calls her "woman". — Verbal act: Naming

E: *Man and woman eat of the fruit of the tree in the middle of the garden.*
1 <u>The serpent asks the woman whether they are not allowed to eat of any tree.</u> — Verbal act: Question
2 Woman replies that they may not eat or touch the tree in the middle of the garden or they will die. — Verbal act: Answer
3 The serpent says that they will not die, but that they will become like God, knowing good and evil. — Verbal act: Answer
4 Woman sees that the tree is good for food and a delight to the eyes. — Sensory/mental act

5	Woman desires the fruit of the tree.	Emotional act
6	<u>Woman takes and eats of its fruit.</u>	Physical act
7	<u>Woman gives some of the fruit to man.</u>	Physical act
8	Man eats some of the fruit.	Physical act
9	They realize that they are naked.	Mental act
10	They sew fig leaves together to make loincloths.	Physical act
F:	*Man and woman hide from God.*	
1	<u>God walks in the garden.</u>	Physical act
2	Man and woman hide themselves.	Physical act
G:	*God and man.*	
1	<u>God calls man.</u>	Verbal act: Question
2	Man replies that he hid himself because he is naked.	Verbal act: Question
3	God asks him who told him that he is naked	Verval act: Question
4	God asks him whether he ate of the tree in the middle of the garden.	Verbal act: Question
5	Man replies that the woman gave it to him and that he ate.	Verbal act: Answer
H:	*God and woman.*	
1	God asks woman what she has done.	Verbal act: Rebuke
2	Woman answers that the serpent tricked her.	Verbal act: Answer
I:	<u>*God curses the serpent.*</u>	
1	God tells the serpent that he will go upon his belly and eat dust.	Verbal act: Curse
2	God tells the serpent that there will be enmity between him and woman.	Verbal act: Curse
J:	<u>*God curses woman.*</u>	
1	God tells woman that her pangs in childbearing will increase greatly.	Verbal act: Curse
2	God tells woman that she will desire for her husband and that he will rule over her.	Verbal act: Curse
K:	<u>*God curses man.*</u>	
1	God tells man that the earth will be cursed.	Verbal act: Curse
2	God tells man that he will eat bread by the sweat of his face until he returns to the ground.	Verbal act: Curse
L:	*Man calls his wife "Eve".*	
1	Man calls his wife "Eve" ("the mother of all living").	Verbal act: Naming
M:	*God clothes man and woman.*	
1	God makes garments of skin for them.	Physical act
2	God clothes them.	Physical act

N:	_God expels man and woman from the garden._	
1	God says that man may also eat from the tree of life	Mental act
2	God expels them from Eden to till the ground	Verbal act: Expulsion
3	God places the cherubim at the garden.	Physical act
4	God places a flaming sword to guard the way to the tree of life.	Physical act

A few comments need to be made:

* Please note that this diagram only provides a summary of the *events* in this narrative. Accordingly those parts that do not recount events, are not included, for example the presentation of the setting in 2:4b-6 and the narrator's commentary in 2:24-25 and 3:1.

* Since this is a representation of the events as narrated in the narrative text, events that are narrated more than once are indicated more than once. See, for example B2 and C1.

* In some instances the classification of acts could possibly be done in another way. This is especially true of some of the actions performed by God. For example: Is C1 a physical act or a verbal act? Is D1 a mental act or a verbal act?

* Some of the verbal acts are more intricate than the classification indicates. A few examples: The serpent's "question" in E1 is not intended as an innocent question, but is a complete distortion of what God said.[19] Similarly woman's "answer" in E2 is more than a simple answer to the serpent's question: She wrongly indicates that God forbade them *to touch the tree* and in this way probably betrays her feelings of discontent.[20] See also man's "answer" to God in G5. This is not simply an answer, but also contains an implied accusation against God himself, since he gave woman to him.[21]

The last issue to be discussed concerns the plot: How is the plot organized in this narrative? In order to discuss this issue I shall present a short overview of the microsequences:

A: God creates man.
B: God creates a garden in Eden.

C: God forbids man to eat of the tree of knowledge of good and evil.
D: God creates woman.
E: Man and woman eat of the fruit of the tree in the middle of the garden.
F: Man and woman hide from God.
G: God and man.
H: God and woman.
I: God curses the serpent.
J: God curses woman.
K: God curses man.
L: Man calls his wife "Eve".
M: God clothes man and woman.
N: God expels man and woman from the garden.

Broadly speaking the plot can be divided into three macrosequences, namely

A-D: Process of improvement
E-K; N: Process of deterioration
L-M: Process of improvement

In the first sequence a definite process of improvement can be detected. The situation as described by the narrator in 2:4b-6 is characterized by a series of lacks: 1. no vegetation, 2. no rain, 3. no-one to till the ground.[22] As the sequence develops, these lacks are resolved one by one.[23] (God even provides man with a partner.) However, note that in the third microsequence in this chain (C) the third lack, the lack of a tiller of the ground, is not only resolved, but a new kernel (C2) is also introduced, which, in Chatman's words, could "force the movement into one of two (or more) possible paths".[24] This happens in the second macrosequence (E-K, N) - clearly is a process of deterioration. From microsequence E to N there is a dramatic change in man and woman's situation: not only in terms of their relationship to God, but also in terms of their relationship to each other, to the animal world, and towards the earth from which they were taken. The whole series of deterioration is started by the serpent's crafty question and finally ends when man and woman find themselves expelled from the garden in Eden. However, significantly, the series of deterioration is interrupted by a short series (consisting of two microsequences only, namely L and M), that I want to typify as a process of improvement. In fact, in God's reaction something along this lines has already been foreshadowed, since, although he cursed man, woman and serpent, he, nevertheless, allowed grace to prevail, since he did not immediately cause them to die. Furthermore, man's action in L should be seen as an act of faith, "an embracing of life, which as a great miracle and mystery is maintained and carried by the motherhood of woman over hardship and death."[25]

That God made them garments of skin (M) is also to be regarded as an act of significance, since God's curses and the expulsion from the garden is somewhat tempered by his role as preserver in this act.[26] Although this short series of improvement cannot reverse the catastrophe that man brought upon himself, it, at least, brings a flicker of light into the darkness.

Which principles are used in the combination of microsequences into macrosequences? To my mind the most important principles are time and causation. *Time* plays a definite role, since the events are narrated in a chronological order. *Causation* plays a role almost everywhere: The series of lacks in 4b-6 causes God to act; God's prohibition causes the serpent to ask woman a question, that, in turn, triggers a disastrous development of events; man and woman's disobedience causes God's actions, etc.

The other principles are used, too, but to a lesser extent. The principle of *character* is used in the sense that at least two of the same constellation of characters are found in each scene: God, man, woman, and the serpent. God is only "absent" from two microsequences (E and L). In the first case events take a catastrophic turn, but in the second case a flicker of hope can be seen. The principle of character can also be detected in the way in which the relationships between characters are changed: From A to D there is harmony, but, thereafter, it is disturbed quite drastically and turns into alienation.[27]

The principle of *space* is used in the sense that all the microsequences are situated in the same location, namely in the garden at Eden. At the end, however, man and woman find themselves outside and barred from the garden.

The principle of *internal relationships* can be indicated in patterns such as the threefold curse (I-K) or the following:[28]

>G: man
>H: woman
>I: serpent
>J: woman
>K: man

There have been some attempts to see this as the most important principle in the organization of the narrative, but I remain doubtful.[29]

The deep structure of events in Gen 2:4b-3:24 will now be discussed. However, before presenting my own analysis of the deep structure, I wish to call attention to the careful and detailed analysis of Ellen van Wolde[30] who distinguishes the following five isotopies:

>1 The relation between God and man
>2 The relation between man and earth
>3 The relation between man and animal
>4 The relation between man and woman
>5 The relation between life and death

In each case she indicates a movement S1 » S2 » S2 » S1. For example, in the case of the first isotopy this movement is as follows: S1: No existence of man apart from God (Gen. 2:4b-6) » S2: Absolute subservience of man to God (Gen. 2:7-25) » S2: Absolute subservience of man to God (Gen. 3:1-7) » S1: Relative autonomy of man in relation to God (Gen. 3:8-24).

In my own representation of the deep structure of Gen. 2:4b-3:24 the same isotopies are important, but I shall organize and describe them in a different way. Since they are closely related to one another, I shall present them in one semiotic square:

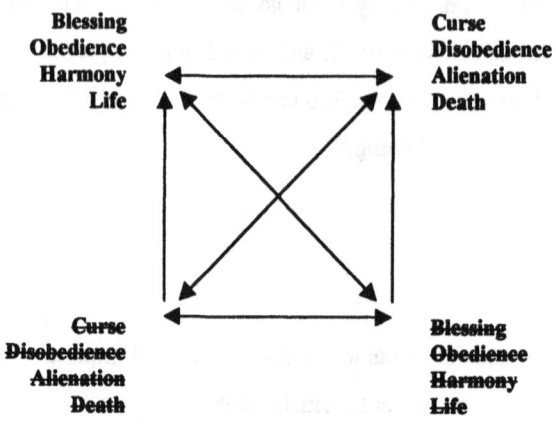

Figure 6

To my mind the movement in the underlying logic is as follows: S1 represents the situation in the narrative world after the creation of man, woman, animals and vegetation (the garden). This situation is characterized by God's blessing, harmony between all the characters, and man's obedient behavior towards God - all of which is a depiction of life in its fullest sense. However, this situation is changed drastically by woman's decision not to be obedient to God's commandment (a movement from S1 to S1̄) resulting in an act of disobedience (S2). The act of disobedience has further implications: God's blessing is replaced by its opposite, namely a threefold curse; harmony (between man and woman, as well as between them and God, the animals and the earth) is replaced by a situation of alienation; and life is shadowed by the reality of death. Fortunately, this is not the end: A last and significant movement can also be detected in the deep structure of the text: God's curses are softened by the fact that the aspect of death is tempered in the sense that man and woman do not die immediately; as well as the prospect of a progressive "chain of life" in spite of death. In the same way the alienation between God and man is softened by God's action of clothing man and woman before expelling them from the garden. Thus, although the wonderful situation depicted in S1 is not attainable any more, at least the possibility of negating God's curse, disobedience, alienation and death is indicated as a possible situation in the deep structure of the narrative.

The second example comes from the New Testament: Acts 27:1-44 (the shipwreck on the way to Rome).

I shall follow the same procedure as in the previous example and first discuss the organization of the surface structure. The following diagram represents the result of the following procedures:

a) A paraphrasing of all the events
b) A classification of all the events
c) An indication of the kernels (underlined)
d) A summary of each microsequence (italics)

A: *The authorities decide to sail for Italy.*
1   The authorities decide to sail for Italy.   Mental act
2   The authorities hand Paul and a few other
    prisoners over to Julius.   Physical act

B: *The party sails to Sidon.*
1   Accompanied by Aristarchus, the party sails
    to Sidon on a ship of Adramyttium.   Physical act
2   At Sidon Julius allows Paul to go to his friends.[31]   Verbal act: Permission

C: *The party sails to Myra in Lycia.*
1   Due to unfavorable winds, the ship sails under
    the lee of Cyprus.   Physical act
2   The ship crosses the sea off Cilicia and Pamphylia.   Physical act
3   The ship reaches Myra.   Physical act

D: *The party sails to Fair Havens near Lasea.*
1   The centurion puts the prisoners on an Alexan-
    drian ship sailing for Italy.   Physical act
2   With difficulty the ship reaches off Cnidus.   Physical act
3   Due to unfavorable winds the ship sails under
    the lee of Crete off Salome.   Physical act
4   With difficulty the ship reaches Fair Havens
    near Lasea.   Physical act

E: *The majority decides to attempt to reach Phoenix.*
1   Paul warns them against the dangers of sailing on

	further: the ship, its cargo, crew and passengers could be endangered.	Verbal act: Warning
2	The centurion ignores Paul.	Mental act
3	The centurion pays more attention to the pilot and the owner of the ship.	Mental act
4	Fair Havens being an unsuitable harbor in which to spend the winter, the majority decides to attempt to reach Phoenix.	Mental act
5	A moderate south wind begins to blow.	Physical act
6	The ship weighs anchor and begins to sail.	Physical act
F:	*A violent wind causes havoc.*	
1	A violent wind, the northeaster, begins to blow.	Physical act
2	The ship is driven around by the wind.	Physical act
3	Near the small island Cauda they succeed in securing the ship's lifeboat.	Physical act
4	They undergird the ship.	Physical act
5	Fearing that they should run on the Syrtis, they let down a drag anchor to act as a brake.	Physical act
6	They throw the cargo overboard.	Physical act
7	They throw the ship's tackle overboard.	Physical act
8	They lose all hope of being saved.	Mental act
G:	*Paul encourages the rest of the party by informing them of a divine revelation he received.*	
1	Paul rebukes them for not having heeded his warning.	Verbal act: Rebuke
2	Paul urges them to keep up their courage.	Verbal act: Encouragement
3	Paul foretells that there will be no loss of life, only of the ship.	Verbal act: Prediction
4	Paul reveals that an angel of God informed him the previous night that he would stand before the emperor and that God had granted safety to all those sailing with him.	Verbal act: Revelation
5	Paul urges them to keep up the courage, since he has faith in God that everything will happen in this way.	Verbal act: Encouragement
6	Paul informs them that they will have to run aground on some island.	Verbal act: Prediction
H:	*The ship runs aground.*	
1	During the fourteenth night (across the sea of Adria) the sailors suspect that they are nearing land.	Mental act
2	The sailors take soundings (twenty fathoms).	Physical act
3	The sailors take soundings (fifteen fathoms).	Physical act
4	The sailors let down four anchors.	Physical act
5	The sailors pray for day to come.	Verbal act: Prayer
6	The sailors try to escape from the ship by using	

	a lifeboat.	Physical act
7	Paul informs the centurion and the soldiers that they will not be saved unless the sailors stay on the ship.	Verbal act: Information
8	The soldiers cut away the ropes of the lifeboat and set it adrift.	Physical act
9	Just before daybreak Paul urges them to take some food for they have not eaten anything for fourteen days.	Verbal act: Advice
10	Paul informs them that none of them will lose a hair from their heads.	Verbal act: Encouragement
11	Paul takes bread.	Physical act
12	Paul gives thanks to God.	Verbal act: Thanksgiving
13	Paul begins to eat.	Physical act
14	The rest of the party begins to eat.	Physical act
15	They throw the wheat into the sea.	Physical act
16	They notice a bay with a beach.	Physical act
17	They attempt to run the ship ashore in the bay.	Physical act
18	The ship strikes a shoal and become immovable.	Physical act
19	The soldiers plan to kill the prisoners.	Mental act
20	The centurion prevents the soldiers from killing the prisoners.	Verbal act: Prohibition
21	He orders everyone who is able to swim, to jump overboard.	Verbal act: Order
22	He orders the rest to follow on planks and other pieces of the ship.	Verbal act: Order
23	Everyone reaches land safely.	Physical act

Two remarks need to be made:

* Note that this diagram only provides a summary of the events in the narrative. Parts that do not refer to events, for example Acts 27:37, are therefore not included.

* In some instances the classification of an event could have been done in another way, since the event may include actions that could be placed under more than one category. For example, in E4 and H19 the events are categorized as "mental acts", but just as well could have been categorized as "verbal acts", since in both cases this is also implied. However, this will have no effect on the discussion of the plot.

In order to discuss the development of the plot in this narrative, a short overview of the microsequences is presented:

A: The authorities decide to sail for Italy.
B: The party sails to Sidon.
C: The party sails to Myra in Lycia.
D: The party sails to Fair Havens near Lasea.
E: The majority decides to attempt to reach Phoenix.
F: A violent wind causes havoc.
G: Paul encourages the rest of the party by informing them of a divine revelation that he received.
H: The ship runs aground.

Broadly speaking the plot can be described as a process of deterioration. Although events take a drastic change only at the sixth microsequence (F: A violent wind causes havoc), the process of deterioration is already suggested in two ways in microsequences C-E:

Firstly, in C1, D2, D3 and D4 it is mentioned that the ship could proceed only very slowly and with difficulty due to unfavorable winds.

Secondly, microsequence E is situated chronologically "after the fast" (Acts 27:9) - an indication that it was an unsafe time to travel by sea.[32] Paul's explicit warning against the dangers of continuing their voyage at this stage suggests that the plot could develop into a process of deterioration.

In the further development of the plot, it becomes clear that the process of deterioration is set in motion because of the wrong (and even foolhardy) choices made by the authorities - in particular the decision made by the centurion, the pilot and the owner of the ship in E4 - a decision that would endanger the cargo, crew and passengers. In fact, apart from this foolhardy decision, Paul's life (together with that of the other prisoners) is endangered at least twice further on: in H6 by the decision of the sailors to escape from the ship and in H19 by the soldiers' plan to kill all the prisoners to prevent them from escaping.

However, it is also important to note that the process of deterioration as such is not the focal point in the development of the plot. The emphasis is placed on the way in which the process of deterioration is softened by God. Microsequence G (Paul encourages the rest of the party by informing them of a divine revelation that he received) could thus be indicated as the focal point in the development of the plot. Since God wants Paul to stand before the emperor in Rome, he will grant safety to everyone on the ship - even though the ship will run aground on an island.

Which principles are used in the combination of the microsequences into a plot? To my mind time, space and causality fulfill an important role. *Time* plays a role in the sense that all the microsequences are linked chronologically. *Space* is used as principle of combination in the sense that the changes in geographical location fulfill an important function. The principle of *causality* is very important, too: The decisions taken by those who are in charge set in motion a movement towards a big catastrophe. This, in turn, leads to the divine intervention.

The last aspect to be discussed is the deep structure of this narrative. To my mind the underlying deep structure of Acts 27 can be reduced to one isotopy, namely the relationship between God and human beings, or more specifically humankind's role in relation to divine planning. Divine planning in Acts 27 can be summarized as follows: Paul must be taken to Rome, but only after the winter. In terms of a semiotic square the various ways in which the isotopy is developed, can then be portrayed as follows:

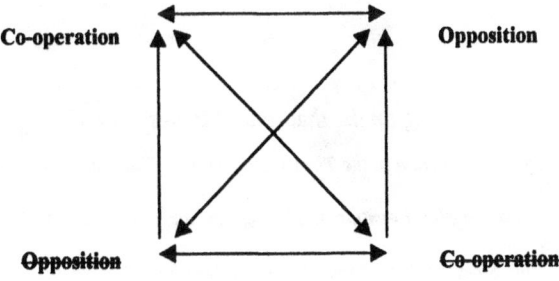

Figure 7

"Co-operation" is represented by Paul who realized that it would not be wise to attempt to sail to Rome at that specific time of year. According to the events narrated in Acts 27, such a situation is characterized by the following: life, order and hope. The contrary relationship "Opposition" is represented in the narrative by the decision of the authorities to sail to Rome - in particular the decision of the centurion, the pilot and the owner of the ship to attempt to reach Phoenix in spite of Paul's warning against such a foolhardy decision (E3,4). The events narrated further on vividly portray the serious consequences of this position: death, chaos and despair. This situation is negated by "~~Opposition~~". In the narrative text this is portrayed in two ways: Firstly, the violent storm reveals all the grave consequences of opposing God's planning, since their desperate situation is characterized by increasing chaos and total despair as a result of the possibility of losing their lives. Secondly, by means of a divine revelation the party is informed that the situation will be changed: In the end no one will die and accordingly there is no need to despair. Thus, in the underlying logic of this narrative we have the following movement: "Opposition" » "~~Opposition~~" » "Co-operation". Significantly, the fourth possibility, "~~Co-operation~~" is left open. In fact, this seems to be the basic message of the narrative: It is not possible not to co-operate in God's plans. Even those who try to oppose God's planning, in the end have to play their part.[33]

Suggestions for further reading on the theoretical issues of analyzing events

Bal, Mieke. *Narratology. Introduction to the Theory of Narrative.* Toronto: University of Toronto Press, 1985: 13-24; 54-67.
Brooks, Peter. *Reading for the Plot. Intention and Design in Narrative.* Oxford: Clarendon, 1984: 3-61.
Caserio, Robert L. *Plot, Story and the Novel From Dickens and Poe to the Modern Period.* Princeton: Princeton University Press, 1979: 3-26.
Chatman, Seymour. *Story and Discourse. Narrative Structure in Fiction and Film.* Ithaca: Cornell, 1986: 43-95.
Cohan, Steven & Shires, Linda M. *Telling Stories. A Theoretical Analysis of Narrative Fiction.* New York: Routledge, 1988: 53-68.

Martin, Wallace. *Recent Theories of Narrative.* Ithaca: Cornell, 1986: 81-99.
Prince, Gerald. *A Dictionary of Narratology.* University of Nebraska Press, 1987.
Rohnen, Ruth. "Paradigm Shifts in Plot Models: An Outline of the History of Narratology", *Poetics Today* 11/4 (1990): 817-842.
Ryan, Mariè-Lauren. *Possible Worlds, Artificial Intelligence and Narrative Theory.* Bloomington: Indiana University Press, 1991: part 2.
Tilley, Allen. *Plot Snakes and the Dynamics of Narrative Experience.* Gainesville: University Press of Florida, 1992.

Suggestions for further reading on the analysis of events in Biblical narratives

Bar-Efrat, Shimon. *Narrative Art in the Bible.* Sheffield: Almond, 1989: 93-140.
Barat, Karen A. "Mission in Matthew. The Second Discourse as Narrative", in *SBL 1988 Seminar Papers*, ed. David J. Lull, (Atlanta: Scholars Press, 1988), 527-535.
Barthes, Roland. *The Semiotic Challenge.* New York: Hill & Wang, 1988: 217-245 ("The Structural Analysis of Narrative Apropos of Acts 10-11"); 246-260 ("Wrestling with the Angel: Textual Analysis of Genesis 32:23-32").
Boers, Hendrikus. *Neither on This Mountain Nor in Jerusalem. A Study of John 4.* Atlanta: Scholars Press, 1988.
Carter, Warren. "Kernels and Narrative Blocks in Matthew", *CBQ* 54/3 (1992): 463-481.
Cooper, Alan. "Narrative Theory and the Book of Job", *SR* 11 (1982): 35-44.
Culley, Robert C. *Themes and Variations. A Study of Action in Biblical Narrative.* Atlanta: Scholars Press, 1997.
Culpepper, R. Alan. *Anatomy of the Fourth Gospel. A Study in Literary Design.* Philadelphia: Fortress, 1983: 86-98.
Green, Barbara. "The Plot of the Biblical Story of Ruth", *JSOT* 23 (1982): 55-68.
Gunn, David M. "The 'Hardening of the Pharaoh's Heart': Plot, Character and Theology in Exodus 1-14", in *Art and Meaning: Rhetoric in Biblical Literature*, eds. David J. A. Clines, David M. Gunn & Alan J. Hauser, (Sheffield: JSOT, 1982), 72-96.
Gunn, David M. & Fewell, Danna Nolan. *Narrative in the Hebrew Bible.* Oxford: Oxford University Press, 1993: 101-146.
Hallberg, Calinda Ellen. "Storyline and Theme in Biblical Narrative: 1 Samuel 3", *OPTAT: Occasional Papers in Translation and Text Linguistics* 3 (1989): 1-35.
Hawk, L. Daniel. *Every Promise Fulfilled. Contesting Plots in Joshua.* Louisville: Westminster, John Knox, 1991.
Humphreys, W. Lee. *Joseph and his Family. A Literary Study.* Columbia: University of South Carolina Press, 1988: 93-117.
Jobling, David. *The Sense of Biblical Narrative. Structural Analysis of the Hebrew Bible.* Two volumes. Sheffield: JSOT, 1986.
Kingsbury, Jack Dean. "The Plot of Matthew", *Interpr* 46/4 (1992): 347-356.
Kunin, Seth D. "The Bridegroom of Blood: A Structural Analysis," *JSOT* 70 (1996): 3-16.
Kurz, William S. *Reading Luke-Acts. Dynamics of Biblical Narrative.* Louisville: Westminster, John Knox, 1993: 17-38.
Lambe, Anthony J. "Genesis 38: Structure and Literary Design", in *The World of Genesis. Persons, Places, Perspectives*, eds. Philip R. Davies & David J. A. Clines, (Sheffield: Sheffield Academic Press, 1998), 102-120.
Matera, Frank J. "The Plot of Matthew's Gospel", *CBQ* 49 (1987): 233-253.
Nicol, George G. "The Narrative Structure and Interpretation of Gen XXVI 1-31," *Vetus Testamentum* 96 (1996): 339-360.

Person, Raymond F. *In Conversation with Jonah: Conversation Analysis, Literary Criticism and the Book of Jonah.* Sheffield: Sheffield Academic Press, 1996: 52-54.
Powell, Mark Allan. "The Plots and Subplots of Matthew's Gospel", *NTS* 38/2 (1992): 187-204.
Resseguie, James L. "John 9: A Literary-Critical Analysis", in *Literary Interpretation of Biblical Narrative. Vol 2*, eds. Kenneth R. R. Gros-Louis & James S. Ackermann, (Nashville: Abingdon, 1982), 295-304.
Rhoads, David & Michie, Donald. *Mark as Story. An Introduction to the Narrative of a Gospel.* Philadelphia: Fortress, 1982: 73-100.
Segovia, Fernando F. "The Journeys of the Word of God. A Reading of the Plot of the Fourth Gospel", *Semeia* 53 (1991): 23-54.
Smith, Stephen H. *A Lion with Wings: A Narrative Critical Approach to Mark's Gospel.* Sheffield: Sheffield Academic Press, 1996: 82-123.
Turner, Laurence A. *Announcements of Plot in Genesis.* Sheffield: JSOT, 1990.
Van Wolde, Ellen J. *A Semiotic Analysis of Genesis 2-3. A Semiotic Theory and Method of Analysis Applied to the Story of the Garden of Eden.* Assen: Van Gorcum, 1989.

Notes

[1] *Telling Stories*, 53-54.
[2] Peter Brooks, *Reading for Plot. Design and Intention in Narrative* (Oxford: Clarendon, 1984), 25.
[3] For more detailed discussions of the syntagmatic and paradigmatic structure of events, see Cohan and Shires, *Telling Stories*, 54-68; as well as Rimmon-Kenan, *Narrative Fiction*, 11-28.
[4] See Rimmon-Kenan, *Narrative Fiction*, 13-28.
[5] *Story and Discourse*, 43-49.
[6] In this regard I follow Wilhelm Wuellner's summary of Chatman, since it is organized better. See Wilhelm Wuellner, "Narrative Criticism and the Lazarus Story", paper read at the Society of New Testament Studies in Rome (Italy), August 1981, 14.
[7] For an example of the use of speech act theory for the classification of events, see my *Farewell*, 101-115.
[8] *Story and Discourse*, 53-54.
[9] Ibid.
[10] Rimmon-Kenan, *Narrative Fiction*, 13-20, only mentions the first two. The rest are added by André P. Brink, *Vertelkunde. 'n Inleiding tot die Lees van Verhalende Tekste* (Pretoria: Academica, 1987), 62-64. For a very useful classification of action sequences in the Hebrew Bible see Robert C. Culley, *Themes and Variations. A Study of Action in Biblical Narrative* (Atlanta: Scholars Press, 1997).
[11] *Narrative Fiction*, 11-15.
[12] See A. J. Greimas, "Elements of a Narrative Grammar", *Diacritics* 7 (1977): 23-40; and A. J. Greimas & J. Courtés, *Semiotics and Language. An Analytical Dictionary* (Bloomington: Indiana University Press, 1982), 132-134.
[13] Ellen J. van Wolde, *A Semiotic Analysis of Genesis 2-3. A Semiotic Theory and Method of Analysis Applied to the Story of the Garden of Eden* (Assen: Van Gorcum, 1989), 61.
[14] David Jobling, *The Sense of Biblical Narrative: Structural Analyses of the Hebrew Bible II* (Sheffield: JSOT Press, 1986), 14.
[15] Cohan and Shires, *Telling Stories*, 67-68.
[16] I follow Van Wolde, *Genesis 2-3*, 125-126, in the definition of the three types of relations.
[17] Ibid., 126.
[18] Due to the complicated editorial process of this narrative one can detect several tensions and

irregularities in it. However, this does not mean that a consistent train of thought cannot be indicated. See Gerhard von Rad, *Genesis. A Commentary*. Revised Edition (London: SCM, 1972), 75:
> No matter how much a knowledge of the previous stages of the present text can preserve us from false exposition, still there is no question that the narrative of chs. 2f., in spite of certain tensions and irregularities, is not a rubble heap of individual recensions but is to be understood as a whole with a consistent train of thought. Above all else the exegete must come to terms with this existing complex unity.

[19] Ibid., 88.
[20] Sternberg, *Poetics*, 391-393.
[21] Bar-Efrat, *Narrative Art*, 206.
[22] See Jobling, *Biblical Narrative*, 23.
[23] However, see Jobling, *Biblical Narrative*, 23-29, for a different view with regard to the lack of some-one to till the (whole) earth.
[24] Chatman, *Story and Discourse*, 53-54.
[25] Von Rad, *Genesis*, 96.
[26] See Claus Westermann, *Genesis 1-11. A Commentary* (Minneapolis: Augsburg, 1974), 269:
> (T)he last action of the creator toward his creature before expelling him from the garden is an action of care and concern ... (T)he creator 'protects' his creatures while putting them at a distance, and the protective action accompanies them on their way.

[27] See Alan John Hauser, "Genesis 2-3: The Theme of Intimacy and Alienation", in *Art and Meaning: Rhetoric in Biblical Literature*, eds. David J. A. Clines, David M. Gunn & Alan J. Hauser, (Sheffield: JSOT Press, 1982), 20-36, for a detailed discussion.
[28] Also see Bar-Efrat, *Narrative Art*, 99.
[29] See, for example, Jerome T. Walsh, "Genesis 2:4b-3:24: A Synchronic Approach", *JBL* 96 (1977): 161-177.
[30] *Genesis 2-3*, especially pages 132-209. For other semiotic analyses, see Jobling, *Biblical Narrative*, 17-43.
[31] The Greek word that is used for "friends" may be a classical designation for Christians. See Ernst Haenchen, *The Acts of the Apostles* (Oxford: Basil Blackwell, 1971), 698.
[32] According to ancient sources the risk of travelling by sea varied with the seasons: 26 May to 14 September (safe season), 14 September to 11 November (risky), 11 November to 10 March (extremely dangerous) and 10 March to 26 May (risky). The events in Acts 27:9 are situated "after the fast", most probably after 5 October in the year 59 A.D. - already in the season considered to be risky for travelling on sea. See Brian M. Rapske, "Acts, Travel and Shipwreck", in *The Book of Acts in its First Century Setting. Volume 2: Graeco-Roman Setting*, eds. Dawid W. J. Gill & Conrad Gempf, (Grand Rapids: Eerdmans, 1994), 22-25.
[33] For an overview of various interpretations of the intention of this narrative, see Rapske, "Shipwreck", 43-46.

CHAPTER SIX

TIME

The analysis of the temporal relations in a narrative text can be one of the most rewarding aspects of a narratological analysis. Gérard Genette[1] provides us with a relatively simple, yet highly effective procedure for analyzing and describing the various ways in which the temporal relations in a narrative text may be manipulated. In this regard he distinguishes three aspects, namely order, duration and frequency. I shall discuss the procedures to be followed in each case and then provide examples from Biblical narratives in order to illustrate the way in which these procedures can be applied to Biblical narratives.

Order

When one analyses the temporal order of a narrative text, one has to compare the order in which the events are arranged in the narrative text with that in which the events originally occurred.[2] For this to be achieved it will be necessary to reconstruct the *original order of events* first - that is, if the events are not narrated in the exact chronological order in which they occurred.

For example, in a narrative text events are narrated in the following order:

Jane's death
Jane's childhood
Jane's school years
Jane's studies at university
Jane's birth
Jane's successful career in advertising
Jane's last years after retirement

If the original order in which these events occurred (the so-called "story level") is reconstructed, it looks as follows:

A: Jane's birth
B: Jane's childhood
C: Jane's school years
D: Jane's studies at university
E: Jane's successful career in advertising
F: Jane's last years after retirement
G: Jane's death

Instead of being narrated in the original order

A B C D E F G

the events were narrated in the following order:

G B C D A E F

Two basic types of "distortion" of temporal order (called "anachronies" by Genette[3]) are illustrated in this example:

Event G (Jane's death) is narrated at a point *before* events that happened earlier, are narrated. This is called a *prolepsis*.

Event A (Jane's birth) is narrated at a point *after* events that happened later, are narrated. This is called an *analepsis*.[4]

In the practical analysis of narrative texts it is essential not only to indicate the various analepses and prolepses, but also to attempt to determine whether there is any reason for the changes that were made by the implied author. This kind of maneuver in narrative texts - particularly the very conspicuous and drastic changes - can be very significant and may sometimes be used to communicate an important ideological perspective.

It may also be helpful to keep the following in mind when analyzing temporal order:

* The implied reader will usually assume that the events are narrated in a chronological order, except when definite indications are given to the contrary. This implies that prolepses and analepses can only be identified as such if they are clearly indicated in some way in the narrative text itself. It is also important to realize that the "original order of events" must be reconstructed from the text and not from other external information or by comparing the text with other texts. This is especially important in the case of Biblical narratives. The "original order" of events should not be confused with the results of historical-critical analyses. Although the historical-critical approach certainly is a valid approach to Biblical texts, the results of historical-critical analyses should not be used in a narratological analysis, since they are based on a completely different approach to the text.

* In some cases the analysis of temporal order can become quite complicated. This often happens when events such as a prophecy or recollection are narrated, since each of these events actually includes two temporal aspects, namely the *act* of prophecy or recollection, and the *content* of prophecy or recollection. For example:

A	On Sunday Paul went to church and spoke to John.
B	On Monday Paul visited his uncle.
C	On Tuesday Paul fell ill.
D	On Wednesday Paul recovered and went to work.
E	On Thursday Paul attended a conference.
F	On Friday Paul remembered that he had spoken to John on Sunday.

A closer analysis of event F reveals that it actually includes two temporal aspects:

On Friday Paul remembered that he had spoken to John on Sunday

            F1   F2

Since F1 is narrated in the narrative text at a stage corresponding to the time at which this event originally occurred, it cannot be classified as an analepsis. In the case of F2 it *seems* as if it may be analeptic since it refers to an event narrated earlier in the narrative. However, this is not an analepsis in the real sense of the word, since the basic action (F1) is not located in a place that differs from its position in the original order of events. In order to distinguish this kind of anachrony from the real cases of anachrony, it may be useful to distinguish between a prolepsis/analepsis and an *embedded* prolepsis/analepsis (such as F above) that, although not proleptic/analeptic themselves, include events that seem to be proleptic/analeptic.[5]

Analepses and prolepses (especially those in the real sense of the word) are not used very often in Biblical narratives. This implies that those that do occur should be scrutinized carefully, since there may be an important reason for their use.

The first example from Biblical narrative comes from the Hebrew Bible. The judgeship of Jephthah is recounted in Judges 10:6-12:7. The events are narrated in the following order:

> *Episode A* (10:6-9): The Israelites abandon the Lord and he delivers them into the hand of the Philistines and the Ammonites.
> *Episode B* (10:10-16): The Israelites put away their foreign gods and start worshipping the Lord again. The Lord responds positively.[6]
> *Episode C* (10:17-18): The Ammonites are called to arms and encamp in Gilead. The commanders of the Israelites are desperate to find a leader.
> *Episode D* (11:1-3): Jephthah's background: Born as the son of a prostitute, Jephthah is driven away by his father's legitimate sons, flees to the land of Tob, where he becomes the leader of a band of outlaws.
> *Episode E* (11:4-11): The elders of Gilead appeal to Jephthah to help them in their war against the Ammonites and he agrees.
> *Episode F* (11:12-28): Jephthah sends messengers to the king of the Ammonites, but he does not heed the message.
> *Episode G* (11:29-31): Jephthah makes a vow to the Lord that if he will give the Ammonites in his hand he will offer whoever comes out of the doors of his house as a burnt offering.
> *Episode H* (11:32-33): Jephthah inflicts a massive defeat on the Ammonites and subdues them.
> *Episode I* (11:34-40): At Jephthah's home his only child, a daughter, comes out to meet him, and (two months later) Jephthah fulfills his vow.
> *Episode J* (12:1-12:6): The men of Ephraim are called to arms to fight against Jephthah and the Gileadites, but Jephthah and his men win the battle.

In this example episode D is an analepsis, since the events narrated in this episode occurred before the events narrated in episodes A-C. If a strict chronological order were followed, episode D would have been narrated first, but, instead, these events are kept back and inserted after episodes A-C. What is the purpose of this analepsis? It seems as if it is used to create a sharp contrast in two ways: Firstly, the contrast between Jephthah as a seasoned and skillful fighter and the confusion amongst the commanders of the Gileadites (episode C) is highlighted.[7] Secondly, a sharp contrast is created between Jephthah's rejection and debasement in this episode and the honor done to him in the next episode when the elders of Gilead ask him to return and promise to make him their leader.[8]

The second example comes from the Second Book of Samuel. In 2 Samuel 17:24-18:33 the war between David and Absalom is narrated. In 2 Samuel 18:9-16 the narrator tells how Absalom was killed by Joab: Absalom's hair caught fast in an oak tree and he was left hanging between heaven and earth. When Joab was informed about this, he took three spears and thrust them into Absalom's heart. This is followed by verses 17 and 18:

> They took Absalom, threw him into a great pit in the forest, and raised over him a very great heap of stones. Meanwhile all the Israelites fled to their homes. Now Absalom in his lifetime had taken and set up for himself a pillar that is in the King's Valley, for he said, "I have no son to keep my name in remembrance"; he called the pillar by his own name ...

In this example verse 18 constitutes an analepsis, since the events narrated in this verse took place before the event narrated in the previous verses. The purpose of this analepsis seems to be to contrast in an ironical way the imposing monument Absalom erected in the King's Valley and the final pitiful outcome of his pride.[9] Indeed, this analepsis adds "an atmosphere of deprivation, sadness and loneliness to the narrative".[10]

The third example comes from the New Testament. In the Gospel according to Mark the events in Chapter 6:7-30 are narrated in the following order:

A (6:7-13):	Jesus sends out the twelve disciples.	
B (6:14-16):	The people's opinion of Jesus' identity.	
C (6:17-29):	The death of John the Baptist.	
D (6:30):	The disciples return and report to Jesus.	

In this case event C is analeptic. In event B some of the opinions with regard to Jesus' identity are recounted. He is regarded as John the Baptist who has been raised from the dead, as Elijah or as a prophet like one of the prophets of old. In verse 16 King Herod's opinion is narrated.

> But when Herod heard of it, he said: "John, whom I beheaded has been raised."

This is then followed by event C (the beheading of the Baptist). This happened at an earlier stage in the story time, but is narrated only now and, accordingly, the whole episode (6:17-29) should be classified as an analepsis.

What is the purpose of this analepsis? One's first response would be to answer that it is used to provide the implied reader with information with regard to the way in which John the Baptist died. This is correct, but there is more to it. The skillful placing of the analepsis results in close association of event C with events A, B and D. Accordingly, the following three issues are linked to one another: the disciples' mission, Jesus' identity and the Baptist's death. Since the implied reader has already been provided with the correct information as to Jesus' identity (that he is the Son of God) in Mark 1:1, King Herod's identification of Jesus as the Baptist who has been raised, will not be accepted. However, what will make sense to the implied reader, and what is suggested by the placing of the analepsis is that John the Baptist can be regarded as a forerunner of Jesus - not only in a temporal sense, but also in the sense of being a model of what will happen to Jesus. As Werner H. Kelber[11] points out:

> The passion narrative of John the Baptist (6:17-29) can therefore be perceived as an anticipation of Jesus' own death, and the synchronization of John's death with the disciples' mission becomes intelligible as an analogy to Jesus' death and the beginnings of the apostolic mission. As John's death coincided with the sending out of the disciples-apostles, so will Jesus' death usher in the mission.

TIME 93

The three examples provided thus far are all examples of anachronies in the real sense of the word. In fact, this type of anachrony is not found very often in Biblical narratives. On the other hand, what I called embedded analepses and prolepses are found much more often and even abound in some narratives. A few examples of embedded prolepses in the Gospel according to Matthew illustrate this:

* The prediction of the coming of the Son of Man (10:23; 13:41 and 16:27)
* The three passion predictions (16:21; 17:22ff. and 20:17ff.)
* Jesus' promise to build his church on Peter (16:18ff.)
* Jesus' eschatological discourse in Matthew 24-25.

Duration

Of the three aspects to be analyzed as part of the temporal organization of a narrative text, the analysis of duration (also called the "speed" of a narrative) is the most difficult. In order to analyze this aspect, one has to compare the length of time an event actually took to occur (the so called "story-time") with the length of time devoted to the narration of this event in the narrative text (the so-called "text-time"). Since it is rather difficult to measure both story-time and text-time, Genette[12] suggests that the best option is to indicate story-time in terms of seconds, minutes, hours, days, months or years. In cases where the story-time is not indicated clearly, one usually can estimate it with reasonable certainty. The estimation of text-time is more difficult. Genette suggests that this can be measured in terms of the number of lines or pages used in narrating each event or group of events. Once story-time and text-time have been established, they should be compared in order to determine the slowdowns or accelerations in the narrative text. Five possible types of relationships between story-time (ST) and text-time (TT) can be indicated:[13]

* In the case of a *narrative pause*, narrative time is devoted to the narration of something (for example, a long description of the setting) without a

corresponding segment appearing in the story. This can be indicated as follows: TT = n, ST = 0. Thus, TT infinitely > ST.

* In a *slowdown* the length of text-time devoted to the narration of the event seems to be longer than the length of time that the event took to occur. This can be indicated as follows: TT > ST.

* In the case of *scenic representation*, the duration of events in the narrative text and the duration of events in the story seem to be more or less identical. This can be indicated as TT = ST. Dialogue is usually regarded as the purest form of scenic representation.[14]

* In a *summary* the events in the narrative text are condensed and fill a shorter space in the text than would have been the case if they had been presented by means of scenic representation. This can be indicated as TT < ST.

* In the case of an *ellipsis*, an event is not narrated in the narrative text, although it is clear that it must have occurred in the story level. This can be indicated as TT = 0, ST = n. Thus, TT infinitely < ST.

The following example will illustrate the use of these categories. From a narrative text in which the life of George is narrated, the text-time (TT) and reconstructed story-time (ST) are as follows:

		TT	ST
A	Physical description of Bill	1 page	-
B	School years	2 lines	12 years
C	College studies	3 pages	3 years
D	First marriage	5 lines	15 years
E	Second marriage	6 pages	4 years
F	Row with his son (dialogue)	7 pages	15 minutes
G	Retirement	15 pages	3 years
H	Death	25 pages	10 minutes

In this case A is an example of a narrative *pause*, since 1 page of text-time is devoted to the physical description of Bill without any corresponding segment in the story-time. B and D are examples of *summaries*, since quite a long stretch of story-time is condensed in the narrative text. F is an example of *scenic representation*, since the extensive use of dialogue results in the illusion that story-time and text-time are equal. H is an example of a *slowdown*, since 25 pages of text-time is devoted to an event that only took 10 minutes to occur. Since Bill's birth, as well as his first years before going to school, is not narrated, these can be indicated as *ellipses*.

From this example the following important information can also be gathered:

* It seems as if events E, G and H are regarded as very important by the implied author, since, in comparison to the other events, much more text-time is devoted to the narration of these events.

* It seems as if events B and D are regarded as rather unimportant by the implied reader, since so little text-time is devoted to them, even though they occupy 27 years of Bill's life. A comparison between the text-time devoted to Bill's first marriage (5 lines for 15 years) in comparison to Bill's second marriage (6 pages for 4 years) confirms this impression.

* It seems as if the speed of the narrative is reduced towards the end of the narrative, since more and more time is devoted to shorter and shorter time-spans.

Two examples from Biblical narratives will now be discussed. The first example comes from the Hebrew Bible. In Judges 4 the slaying of Sisera is narrated. The story-time is reconstructed from the narrative text in terms of either years or days. Text-time is indicated in terms of number of lines in *Biblica Hebraica Stuttgartensia* (1984:editio minor).

EVENTS	ST	TT	TECHNIQUE
A. The Canaanites oppress the Israelites (4:1-3).	20 years	4 lines	Summary
B. Deborah as judge (4:4-5).	Indefinite	3 lines	Summary
C. Deborah sends for Barak (4:6a)	Several days	1 line	Summary
D. Deborah instructs Barak to take position at Mount Tabor (4:6b-9c).	1 hour	7 lines	Scene

E. Barak, Deborah and the Israelite warriors go to Kedesh (4:9d-10).	Several days	2 lines	Summary
F. Heber encamps near Kedesh (4:11).	Indefinite	2 lines	Summary
G. Sisera and his troops attack the Israelites, but are beaten. Sisera flees by foot (4:12-16).	One day	8 lines	Summary
H. Sisera reaches Jael's tent. She invites him into her tent and gives him milk. Sisera falls asleep and Jael kills him driving a peg into his temple (4:17-21).	1 hour	9 lines	Scene
I. Jael shows Sisera's body to Barak (4:22).	Few minutes	2 lines	Scene
J. King Jabin of Canaan is destroyed (4:23-24).	Several years	2 lines	Summary

This example illustrates some of the problems one encounters when analyzing duration in narrative texts - especially with regard to the reconstruction of the story-time. Sometimes the exact length of the story-time is indicated in the narrative, for example in the case of event A (twenty years), but quite often one cannot indicate the story-time accurately, for example in the case of events C, E and G. Nevertheless, the over-all picture provides some interesting results:

1. In total the length of the story-time portrayed in the narrative is more or less thirty years. This is portrayed mostly by means of summaries. The only exceptions are events D, H and I which are portrayed by means of scenic representation. Although these three scenes depict only about two hours out of a total of 30 years' story-time, 18 out of 40 lines, that is 45% of the text-time is devoted to the narration of these events. This is a clear indication of the

importance attached to these events by the implied author.

2. The narrative is organized in such a way that the speed of the narrative is reduced towards the end of the narrative. Events H and I are portrayed by means of scenic representation. In the case of event H the slowing down of the narrative speed is remarkable. The actions are narrated individually: Jael invites Sisera in a friendly manner; he turns aside into her tent; she covers him with a rug; he asks for water; she opens a skin of milk; gives him a drink and covers him; he asks her to stand at the entrance of the tent and to pretend that he is not there; he falls asleep; she takes a tent peg; she takes a hammer; she drives the peg into his temple until it goes into the ground; and Sisera dies. In this way the implied author succeeds in expanding the text-time precisely at the moment that the decisive deed is narrated.[15]

The second example comes from the New Testament. I shall provide an analysis of the way in which duration is handled in the Gospel according to John.[16] Since Alan Culpepper[17] has already done important research in this regard, I shall firstly point out some of his results:

* The temporal structure of the Gospel is dominated by scenes connected by means of summaries or ellipses. The oscillation between scenes (usually involving confrontation) and summaries (usually referring to withdrawals by Jesus) serves to give a rhythmic nature to the narrative.

* The time span of the story covers a period of about two and a half years. It starts with the gathering of the disciples and ends with the resurrection appearances of Jesus. From this period, events covering about two months are narrated in the narrative text.

* As far as the first year is concerned, events covering about two weeks are narrated in 116 verses in the narrative text, and of the second year events covering about a month are narrated in 295 verses in the narrative text.

* In John 13-20 the speed of the narrative is reduced dramatically, virtually grinding to a halt during the events of Jesus' hour.

In order to discuss the way in which duration is handled in this Gospel I provide a table, summarizing text-time and story-time. Story-time is measured in terms of days/evenings - in so far as it is possible to determine this from the narrative text. Although events usually take up only a small part of a day or an evening, they are indicated in the summary in terms of days/evenings. In those cases where no clear indications are given in the text, or where the divisions within the text are not clearly indicated, this is indicated by means of a question mark. Text-time is measured in terms of the number of lines devoted to each event as it is printed in Nestle-Aland's *Novum Testamentum Graece* (1988: 26th edition, 10th impression).

PASSAGE		STORY-TIME	TEXT-TIME
1:1-18	Prologue	-	39
1:19-28	John's testimony	1 day	19
1:29-34	John's testimony	1 day	13
1:35-51	The first disciples	2 days	37
2:1-11	The sign at Cana	1 day	21
2:12	Capernaum	A few days (?)	3
2:13-22	Cleansing of the temple	1 day	21
2:23-25	Jerusalem	A few days (?)	21
3:1-21	Nicodemus	1 evening	44
3:22	Jesus in Judea	A few days (?)	2
3:23-35	John's testimony	1 day	27
4:1-39	Jesus and the Samaritan woman	1 day	78
4:40-42	Jesus and the Samaritans	2 days	4
4:43-54	The second sign at Cana	1 day	26
5:1-47	The sign at Bethesda	1 day	92
6:1-21	Multiplication of the loaves	1 day	41
6:22-71	Bread from heaven	1 day (?)	92
7:1-9	Unbelieving brothers	1 day	16
7:10-52	Festival of the Tabernacles	2 days (?)	82
8:12-20	Temple treasury	1 day	19
8:21-59	Discourse: Jews	1 day (?)	80
9:1-10:21	Man born blind	1 day	125
10:22-39	Festival of dedication	1 day	32
10:40-42	Withdrawal	A few days (?)	5
11:1-44	Lazarus	4 days	81

11:45-50	Decision to kill Jesus	A few days	30
12:1-11	Anointing	1 day	23
12:12-19	Entrance into Jerusalem	1 day	17
12:20-36	The coming of the hour	1 day (?)	36
12:37-43	Results of Jesus' works	-	13
12:44-52	Another discourse	1 day (?)	14
13:1-17:26	Situation of farewell	1 evening	313
18:1-19:42	Arrest/trial/crucifixion	Rest of the night and next day	189
20:1-18	At the tomb	1 day (morning)	39
20:19-23	First appearance	1 evening	10
20:24-29	Second appearance	1 day	15
20:30-31	Purpose of Gospel	-	5
21:1-22	Sea of Tiberias	1 day	53
21:23-25		Conclusion	9

From this summary it is clear that John 13:1-17:26 forms the largest single episode within the Gospel: Out of a total of 1786 lines covering two and a half year's story-time, 313 lines (17,5%) are devoted to events that happened in a single evening! Even more lines are used to cover these events than for the arrest, trial and crucifixion (189 lines/10,5%). This can be interpreted as a clear indication of the importance attached to these events, since ordinarily the more important events are narrated in more detail.[18] It may thus be stated that the surprisingly large amount of text-time devoted to the narration of the events in John 13:1-17:26 serves as a clear indication of the importance of these events in comparison to other events in the Gospel. Furthermore, Culpepper's[19] statement that the speed of the narrative virtually grinds to a halt during the events of Jesus' hour can be reformulated in a slightly different way. The speed of the narrative virtually grinds to a halt during the evening before the crucifixion, after which it accelerates - although the speed of the narrative is still much slower than in John 1-12.

Frequency

In order to analyze the temporal aspect "frequency", the issue that should be investigated is the relation between the number of times an event occurs in the "story level" and the number of times it is narrated in the narrative text. In this regard Genette[20] distinguishes between three kinds of frequency:

* *Singulative frequency*: In the case of singulative frequency, a one-to-one relationship exists between the events in the story level and the events in the narrative text. Two types of singulative frequency can be distinguished: an event that happened once is narrated once; or the same kind of event that happened more than once is narrated a corresponding number of times.

* *Repetitive frequency*:[21] What happened once, is narrated more than once in the narrative text.

* *Iterative frequency*: What happened more than once, is narrated once in the narrative text.

For example, a number of events originally occurred as follows:

    A B1 C B2 D B3 E B4 F G
    (B1, B2, B3 and B4 represent multiple occurrences of the same kind of event, for example, eating breakfast every morning.)

If these events are narrated as follows:

    A B1-4 C D C E C F G,

A, D, E, F and G are examples of singulative frequency, B of iterative frequency and C of repetitive frequency.

In the case of Biblical narratives singulative frequency and iterative frequency are used quite often. That the dominant pattern in Biblical narratives is singulative frequency can be seen from all the examples discussed so far in this chapter. Iterative frequency is also used to some extent - usually to indicate a particular pattern in the lives of characters. Four examples are provided:

1 Samuel 1:3

> Now this man (= Elkanah) used to go up year by year from his town to worship and to sacrifice to the Lord of hosts at Siloh, where the two sons of Eli, Hophni and Pinehas, were priests of the Lord.

Daniel 6:10

Although Daniel knew that the document had been signed, he continued to go to his house, which had windows in its upper room open toward Jerusalem, and to get down on his knees three times a day to pray to his God and to praise him, just as he had done previously.

Luke 2:41

Now every year his (= Jesus') parents went to Jerusalem for the festival of the Passover.

Acts 2:44-47

Awe came upon everyone, because many wonders and signs were being done by the apostles. All who believed were together and had all things in common; they would sell their possessions and goods and distribute the proceeds to all, as any had need. Day by day, as they spent much time together in the temple, they broke bread at home and ate their food with glad and generous hearts, praising God and having the goodwill of all the people. And day by day the Lord added to their number those who were being saved.

Suggestions for further reading on the analysis of temporal relations in narrative texts

Bal, Mieke. *Narratology. Introduction to the Theory of Narrative.* Toronto: University of Toronto Press, 1985: 37-43
Chatman, Seymour. *Story and Discourse. Narrative Structure in Fiction and Film.* Ithaca: Cornell, 1978: 63-78.
Cohan, Steven & Shires, Linda M. *Telling Stories. A Theoretical Analysis of Narrative Fiction.* New York: Routledge, 1988: 83-89.
Genette, Gérard. *Narrative Discourse.* Oxford: Basil Blackwell, 1984: 33-160.
Genette, Gérard. *Narrative Discourse Revisited.* Ithaca: Cornell University Press, 1988: 21-40.
Martin, Wallace. *Recent Theories of Narrative.* Ithaca: Cornell, 1986: 74-76, 86-87; 120-139.
Prince, Gerald. *A Dictionary of Narratology.* University of Nebraska Press, 1987.
Rimmon-Kenan, Shlomith. *Narrative Fiction. Contemporary Poetics.* London: Metheuen, 1983: 43-58.

Suggestions for further reading on the analysis of temporal relations in Biblical narratives

Bal, Mieke. *Lethal Love. Feminist Literary Readings of Biblical Love Stories.* Bloomington: Indiana University Press, 1987: 89-103.
Bar-Efrat, Shimon. *Narrative Art in the Bible.* Sheffield: Almond Press, 1989: 141-183.
Culpepper, R. Alan. *Anatomy of the Fourth Gospel. A Study in Literary Design.* Philadelphia: Fortress, 1983: 51-76.
Claassens, L. M. J. "Notes on Characterisation in the Jephtah Narrative", *Journal of North West Semitic Languages* 22/2 (1996): 107-115 (in particular 110-111).

Funk, Robert W. *The Poetics of Biblical Narrative*. Sonoma: Polebridge, 1988: 187-206.
Holleran, J. Warren. "Narrative Reading of John", *EThL* 69/1 (1993): 21-22.
Howell, David B. *Matthew's Inclusive Story. A Study in the Narrative Rhetoric of the First Gospel*. Sheffield: JSOT Press, 1990: 93-160.
Licht, Jacob. *Storytelling in the Bible*. Jerusalem: Magnes Press, 1978: 96-120.
O'Day, Gail R. "'I have Overcome the World' (John 16:33): Narrative Time in John 13-17", *Semeia* 53 (1991): 153-166.
Powell, Mark Allen. *What is Narrative Criticism?* Minneapolis: Fortress, 1990: 35-43.
Reinhartz, Adele. "Jesus as Prophet: Predictive Prolepses in the Fourth Gospel", *JSNT* 36 (1989): 3-16.
Schildgren, Brenda Deen. *Crisis and Community. Time in the Gospel of Mark*. Sheffield: Sheffield Academic Press, 1998: 94-116.
Smith, Stephen H. *A Lion with Wings: A Narrative-Critical Approach to Mark's Gospel*. Sheffield: Sheffield Academic Press, 1996: 124-150.

Notes

[1] See his *Narrative Discourse* and *Narrative Discourse Revisited*.

[2] Genette, *Narrative Discourse*, 35-85.

[3] Ibid. See also Rimmon-Kenan, *Narrative Fiction*, 46-51.

[4] Genette, *Narrative Discourse*, 35ff., also distinguishes between external and internal analepsis/prolepsis, heterodiegetic and homodiegetic analepsis/prolepsis, and completing and repeating analepsis/prolepsis. These are not discussed, since too many distinctions may become confusing to a beginner.

[5] For a more detailed discussion of this aspect, see my *Jesus' Farewell*, 151-153.

[6] See Barry G. Webb, *The Book of Judges. An Integrated Reading* (Sheffield: SJOT Press, 1987), 45-46.

[7] Webb, *The Book of Judges*, 50-51.

[8] Bar-Efrat, *Narrative Art*, 175-176.

[9] Ibid., 178.

[10] See Jan P. Fokkelman, *Narrative Art and Poetry in the Books of Samuel. Volume 1: King David. Full Interpretation Based on Stylistic and Structural Analyses* (Assen: Van Gorcum, 1981), 249.

[11] *Mark's Story*, 34.

[12] *Narrative Discourse*, 86-112. See also his *Narrative Discourse Revisited*, 33-37.

[13] Genette, *Narrative Discourse*, 94-95, actually distinguishes only four categories. The fifth category ("slowdown") is distinguished by Bal, *Narratology*, 71.

[14] See Rimmon-Kenan, *Narrative Fiction*, 54. It is important to realize that the supposed equality between story-time and text-time is only an illusion. See Jakob Licht, *Storytelling*, 97, in this regard:

> Scenes are always slower than straight narrative, and are occasionally defined as those passages in which telling time is slowed down enough to appear equal to action time. The definition can be misleading. In many scenes the difference between action time and telling time remains in fact considerable; what matters is that the *telling tempo* is noticeably slower in scenes than in the passages of straight narrative that frame them.

[15] Licht, *Storytelling*, 103.

[16] From my *Jesus' Farewell*, 157-161.

[17] *Anatomy*, 70-73.
[18] This can also be illustrated from modern fiction: In his analysis of *Recherche du temps perdu*, Genette, *Narrative Discourse*, 92, uses the same procedure and indicates important variations in the speed of the narrative, such as 150 pages devoted to three hours, and three lines devoted to 12 years. Rimmon-Kenan, *Narrative Fiction*, 6-57, cites Flaubert's *Sentimental Education* as an example: Some 400 pages are used to cover a period of 11 years, whereas 16 years are compressed into a dozen lines.
[19] *Anatomy*, 70-73.
[20] *Narrative Discourse*, 113-116.
[21] In the translation of Genette's *Narrative Discourse*, 117, the word "repeating" is used, but I prefer the term "repetitive" that is used by Rimmon-Kenan, *Narrative Fiction*, 57.

CHAPTER SEVEN

SETTING

Just as no narrative can exist without characters or events, no narrative can be imagined without a setting: no narrative can be imagined without the events occurring *somewhere at some specific point in time*. Of course, a narrative can be narrated in such a way that absolutely no information is provided to the implied reader with regard to the place[1] or the exact point in at which the events occurred. Nevertheless, even if this is the case, the implied reader will attempt to create some sort of mental image of the setting - even though it may be quite vague.

In this chapter we shall consider the analysis of the setting in Biblical narratives. It is important to note that this discussion will be restricted to the setting of the events in the narrated world only. The issue of the spatial and chronological orientation of narrators was already considered earlier on (see pages 13-16) and will not be repeated.

Analyzing settings in Biblical narratives

Basically one has to consider two issues when one analyzes the setting of events in Biblical narratives. I shall discuss them shortly:

1. Does the implied author provide any information regarding the setting, and if so, how is this communicated to the implied reader?

The implied author has two ways in which it can provide information on the setting to the implied reader. First of all such information can be provided directly (by the narrator or by one of the characters). For example, in Daniel 7:1 the implied author uses the narrator to describe the setting as follows:

> In the first year of King Belshazzar of Babylon, Daniel had a dream and visions in his head as he lay in bed...

The second procedure that can be followed is to convey the information to the implied reader in an indirect way. This can be achieved by mentioning certain objects, actions or conditions that will immediately suggest a certain setting to the implied reader. For example, in Mark 1:40-44 the implied author does not provide any description of the setting. The narrator only mentions that a person with leprosy came to Jesus. Based on this information the implied reader will be able to reconstruct a vague spatial setting. Since the implied reader knows that persons with leprosy were not allowed to come into the cities or villages,[2] it will imagine a vague setting somewhere outside a city.

2. Is there any significance in the setting that is provided?

In most cases in Biblical narratives the only function of the setting is to provide the implied reader with information as to where and when the narrated events occurred. However, this should not leave you the under the impression that the setting can be neglected in a narratological analysis. In some cases the setting is highly significant and therefore it may be worthwhile to investigate the setting very carefully - in particular in longer narratives where quite a number of different settings are used. The following questions may be helpful:

* Is the setting directly relevant to the rest of the narrative?
* Can any symbolic connotations be attached to the setting?
* Can a pattern of movement be detected? If so, does it have any significance?
* Are any positive or negative feelings associated with a particular setting?

Settings in Biblical narratives

In order to illustrate the significance of settings in some Biblical narratives, I shall discuss a few examples. The settings in the Hebrew Bible will be considered first. I shall first make some general remarks with regard to the way in which settings are used in the Hebrew Bible and thereafter discuss one example in more detail.

The following general remarks can be made with regard to the way in which settings are used in the Hebrew Bible:[3]

* In most cases the setting is provided by the narrator. Only very rarely is this done by other characters.

* The spatial setting is shaped mostly by reference to places and the movement of characters, for example, journeys.

* Places such as cities, villages, rivers, streams, wells, mountains or forests are mentioned frequently. These are usually mentioned as an integral part of the plot of the narratives.

* When characters are travelling, usually only the place that the character leaves and the one s/he reaches, is mentioned, without any discussion of the territory in between.

* Places are usually not depicted clearly and vividly. The setting is usually merely portrayed as the background against which the action takes place, but no detailed or graphic descriptions are provided. The physical environment is usually not described at all - not even its general outline.

As an example of the significance that a setting may have in the Hebrew Bible, the setting of the Book of Deuteronomy can be pointed out. The narrative is structured mainly as a series of speeches by Moses. In Deuteronomy 1:1-5 the setting of these speeches is provided by the narrator:

> (1) These are the words that Moses spoke to all Israel beyond the Jordan - in the wilderness, on the plain opposite Suph, between Paran and Tophel, Laban, Hazeroth, and Di-zahab. (2) (By the way of Mount Seir it takes eleven days to

reach Kadesh-barnea from Horeb.) (3) In the fortieth year, on the first day of the eleventh month, Moses spoke to the Israelites just as the Lord had commanded him to speak to them. (4) This was after he had defeated King Sihon of the Amorites, who reigned in Heshbon, and King Og of Bashan, who reigned in Ashtaroth and in Edrei. (5) Beyond the Jordan in the land of Moab, Moses undertook to expound this law as follows...

The significance of this setting becomes clear if the following is considered:[4]

* Why are the date and place fixed so carefully in verses 1 and 3? It serves as an indication of the importance of the events that are about to take place. This is the day of Israel's decision to enter the Promised Land - a well-known juncture in the history of Israel.

* At first glance the parenthesis in verse 2 seems to be rather odd and out of place. However, one should realize that the parenthesis is not used primarily to point out geographical details, but to remind the implied reader of Kadesh-barnea and *what happened there*. More or less forty years previously the Israelites had rebelled at Kadesh-barnea. They were afraid to enter the Promised Land, since ten of the twelve spies had reported that it would be too dangerous to enter the land. God's judgment was that they would be forced to wait another forty years before they could enter the Promised Land. The parenthesis in verse 2 is used to point out the irony: if the Israelites had trusted God at Kadesh-barnea they could have reached this place after eleven days only. Instead they had to wait another forty years. What follows in the narrative is thus portrayed as either a possible chance to repair the mistake of Kadesh-barnea or a possible repetition of the old mistake.

* The victories over King Sihon and King Og (verse 4) are mentioned not only as a chronological marker, but also to point out the possibilities for success in spite of the disaster at Kadesh-barnea.

Before moving on to the New Testament I shall make a few remarks on the significance of *mountains* as settings in the Hebrew Bible. Robert L. Cohn[5] identifies the three major foci of mountain imagery in the Hebrew Bible. Although his study is not restricted to narrative material alone, the results of his research can be kept in mind in the analysis of narratives in the Hebrew Bible, as well as in the New Testament. The three foci are as follows:

* Mountains are renowned for their *security*. They often serve as hiding places for fugitives (for example, Judges 6:2). They may also be associated with the protection of Yahweh (for example, Psalm 121:1). In Biblical cosmology they stand as a firm testimony to the orderliness of creation (for example, Psalm 65:6) and may be singled out for their antiquity (for example, Job 15:7). However, in the depiction of Yahweh's wrath (for example, Psalm 97:5) it is said that even the mountains will not be able to stand before him.

* Mountains are impressive because of their *height* (physical dimensions). Accordingly they are quite often associated with authority. Certain mountains, such as Mount Sinai, Mount Gerizim or Mount Ebal fulfill a very important function in some Biblical narratives. Similarly, mountain tops are often used as places from which divine pleasure or anger is conveyed, for example Judges 9:7. Mountain tops may be used as settings for the pronouncement either of curses (for example, 2 Chronicles 13:4-12) or of blessings (such as in the Balaam stories). Another interesting use of the mountain settings is the way in which they may be associated with human pride and arrogance, for example, Obadiah 3 or the "artificial mountain" built in the story of Tower of Babel.

* Mountains may also be associated with *fertility*. In a positive sense they are perceived as the foremost features of the fertility of the promised land (for example, Deuteronomy 11:11). In a negative sense mountains may also serve as settings for illicit sexual rites as practiced by some of the pagan cults (for example, Hosea 4:13f).

We shall consider two examples from the New Testament. In the Gospel according to Luke, the settings are used in the following way:[6]

* With regard to the *chronological setting*, the life of Jesus is situated within

the broader context of Palestinian history in order to link Jesus to world history.

* With regard to the way in which *spatial settings* are used in the Gospel according to Luke several interesting aspects can be indicated:

- *Galilee* is the place where Jesus begins his ministry, where he presents himself to Israel as God's Messiah and from where he reaches out to all Israel. It is also the place where he selects the twelve disciples and other people to follow him.

- The *desert* is portrayed as a place of isolation, but also of eschatological renewal. Examples: John the Baptist lives in the desert until he is called by God (1:80). The desert areas in the Jordan Valley are also the place where John the Baptist starts preaching his message. In the Gospel according to Luke the desert is also portrayed as a place where Satan and other demons are to be found (4:1), where one can go for prayer and communion with God (5:16), and where God provides miraculously through Jesus.

- The *lake* is portrayed in two opposite ways. On the one hand it is the place where the disciples catch so many fish that their boats start to sink (Luke 5:4-7). On the other hand it is also the place where their unbelief and ignorance of Jesus' identity come to the fore (Luke 8:22-25).

- The *synagogue* is the special place of the Jewish religious leaders (scribes and Pharisees). It is also the place in which Jesus proclaims the good message (Luke 4:14-15; 4:44), where he is rejected (Luke 4:16-30) and performs controversial deeds (Luke 6:6-11; 13:10-17).

- The *mountain* is portrayed as a place denoting nearness to God and security. Jesus prays on a mountain (Luke 6:12; 9:28; 22:39) and is transfigured there (9:29-36). In Luke 21:21 Jesus advises his followers to flee to the mountains for refuge during the final days.

- *Jerusalem* fulfills a very important role in the narrative. It is the city in which God chose to dwell, where his temple is to be found and, as such it constitutes the center of Israel. The temple is portrayed as a place of prayer, instruction and praise of God. People who are really pious, such as Simeon (Luke 2:25-35), Anna (Luke 2:36-40) and the poor widow (Luke 21:1-4) are portrayed in the temple. Luke's narrative mainly begins in the temple in Jerusalem, thereby indicating that God's new actions form a continuity with his past actions. As the story develops, the portrayal of Jerusalem changes as it also becomes symbolic of Israel's rejection of Jesus. After the transfiguration (Luke 9:28-36) Jesus begins his long journey to Jerusalem that takes up most of the rest of the narrative (Luke 9:51-19:46). The implied reader is reminded repeatedly throughout this journey that Jesus' final goal is Jerusalem where he has to suffer and die (Luke 9:53; 13:22; 13:33; 17:11; 17:25; 18:31-33 and 19:28). At his arrival in Jerusalem Jesus clashes with the Jewish religious authorities, suffers and is finally crucified. Hereafter the portrayal of Jerusalem is changed again. After the resurrection it becomes the place from which the good news will be spread throughout the whole world (Luke 24:47, see also Acts 1:8).

* With regard to the way in which the implied author employs *social* settings, one typical setting can be pointed out. Five times the implied reader uses type-scenes where Jesus is found at a meal. In three of these scenes Jesus is portrayed with tax collectors and other "sinners". This provokes a response from the Pharisees and scribes (they "grumble") giving Jesus occasion to silence them. In the other two scenes Jesus is portrayed as having a meal in the home of a Pharisee when something controversial happens, thereby giving Jesus occasion to criticize either his host or the other Pharisees.

As a second example from the New Testament the way in which settings are employed in the Gospel according to Mark will be discussed. Some of these settings (for example, Jerusalem) is used more or less in the same way as in the

Gospel according to Luke and will not be discussed again. I list some of the settings in order to show the significance attached to them:[7]

* John the Baptist's activity at the *Jordan river* signals a new beginning, preparing the way for the Lord.

* The *sea* is portrayed as a place of chaos and destruction: it is a place into which someone is to be thrown with a millstone tied around his neck, where two thousand pigs together with the demons in them are destroyed, where a storm threatens the lifes of Jesus and the disciples. However, it is also a setting where Jesus can demonstrate his authority by stopping the wind, calming the sea and later walking on it.

* *Private settings*, for example in a house, a boat or on a mountain, are used to create privacy for Jesus and his disciples. These are also used as settings for private teaching to the disciples, and in this way contribute to the secrecy motif in the Gospel, since only the characters present at these settings know what happens here. Furthermore the private settings also serve as settings for the conflict between Jesus and his disciples.

* *Public settings* (synagogues and the temple) are not only used as settings for demonstrating Jesus' authority, but also function as focal points in the growing conflict between Jesus and the religious leaders.

* The *pattern of movement* in the Gospel according to Mark is very significant. Jesus changes setting more than forty times in the narrative - thereby underscoring the urgency of his message, his success and the bigger goal that he has in mind. The setting "beside the sea" is also very significant: This is the place where Jesus calls the first four disciples. Later, when he returns, a huge crowd follows him. Still later an even larger crowd (not only from Galilee, but also from Judea, Jerusalem, Idumea, across the Jordan and around Tyre and Sidon) follows him. When Jesus is again depicted beside the sea, the crowd is so huge that he is

forced to get into a boat in order to teach them.

* Jesus is often depicted in *Gentile territory* (Tyre, Sidon, and the region of the ten cities across the Sea of Galilee). In these territories Jesus is very popular and more or less the same pattern as in Galilee can be indicated: Great popularity and yet intense opposition from some quarters which prompts Jesus to withdraw; healing and preaching which draw even larger crowds leaving Jesus with virtually no privacy at all.

Suggestions for further reading on the theoretical aspects of analyzing settings

Chatman, Seymour. *Story and Discourse. Narrative Structure in Fiction and Film.* Ithaca: Cornell, 1978: 96-106
Kenney, William. *How to Analyze Fiction.* New York: Monarch Press, 1966: 38-45.
Macauley, Robie & Lanning, George. *Technique in Fiction.* New York: Harper & Row, 1964: 119-139.
Prince, Gerald. *Narratology. The Form and Functioning of Narrative.* Berlin: Mouton, 1982: 31-33.
Rimmon-Kenan, Shlomith. *Narrative Fiction. Contemporary Poetics.* London: Metheuen, 1983: 66-70; 96-97.
Smitten, Jeffrey R. & Daghistany, Ann. Eds. *Spatial Form in Narrative.* Ithaca: Cornell, 1981.

Suggestions for further readings on the analysis of settings in Biblical narratives

Bar-Efrat, Shimon. *Narrative Art in the Bible.* Sheffield: Almond, 1989: 141-195.
Cohn, Robert L., *The Shape of Sacred Space: Four Biblical Studies.* Chico: Scholars Press, 1981.
Fields, Weston F. *Sodom and Gomorrah. History and Motif in Biblical Narrative.* Sheffield: Sheffield Academic Press, 1997: 86-115.
Holleran, J. Warren. "Seeing the Light. A Narrative Reading of John 9", *EThL* 93/1 (1993): 5-26.
Malbon, Elizabeth Struthers. "The Jesus of Mark and the Sea of Galilee", *JBL* 103/3 (1984): 363-377.
Malbon, Elizabeth Struthers. *Narrative Space and Mythic Meaning in Mark.* San Francisco: Harper & Row, 1986.
Noegel, Scott B. "A Crux and a Taunt: Night Time Then Sunset in Genesis 15", in *The World of Genesis. Persons, Places, Perspectives,* eds. Philip R. Davies & David J. A. Clines, (Sheffield: Sheffield Academic Press, 1998), 128-135.
Powell, Mark Allan. *What is Narrative Criticism?* Minneapolis: Fortress, 1990: 70-84.
Rhoads, David & Michie, Donald. *Mark as Story. An Introduction to the Narrative of a Gospel.* Philadelphia: Fortress, 1983: 62-73.
Van Iersel, Bas. "Locality, Structure and Meaning in Mark", *LingBib* 53 (1983): 45-54.

Notes

[1] See Prince, *Narratology*, 32-33.
[2] People with leprosy had to live alone outside the city and often begged at the city gate during the daytime hours. See Bruce J. Malina & Richard L. Rohrbaugh, *Social Science Commentary on the Synoptic Gospels* (Minneapolis: Fortress, 1992), 70.
[3] These remarks are based on the detailed discussion of Bar-Efrat, *Narrative Art*, 184-196.
[4] The following discussion is based on the study by J. G. McConville & J. G. Millar, *Time and Place in Deuteronomy* (Sheffield: Sheffield Academic Press, 1994) - in particular pp. 23-24. J.G. Millar discusses Chapters 1-11 and 27-34 and J.G. McConville discusses the Deuteronomic Altar-Law in Deuteronomy 12. Note that I discuss only the setting in Deuteronomy 1. Time and place also play an important role in the rest of the narrative as McConville and Millar indicate.
[5] *The Shape of Sacred Space: Four Biblical Studies* (Chico: Scholars Press, 1981), 29-38.
[6] The following discussion is based on Jack Dean Kingsbury, *Conflict in Luke*, 4-8.
[7] The following discussion is based on Rhoads & Michie, *Mark as Story*, 63-72.

CHAPTER EIGHT

IMPLIED AUTHOR AND IMPLIED READER

In the previous chapters I discussed various individual aspects that are considered important when attempting a narratological analysis. Now it remains to indicate how one could go about *integrating* the results of the various individual analyses. To my mind, the best way to achieve this, is to integrate the results of the various analyses in terms of the relation between the implied author and the implied reader. In the first chapter, I discussed both concepts and defined both of them in a depersonified way. The *implied author* was defined in terms of the *overall textual strategy*, thus including all the aspects discussed in Chapters 2-7: narrator and narratee, focalization, characters, events, time and setting. The *implied reader* was defined as the *counterpart of the implied author*. I also pointed out that the difference between these concepts should be described in terms of the difference between the *linearity* (implied author) and the *temporality* (implied reader) of the text. Whereas the implied author is defined as the overall textual strategy in the sense of a static overarching view of the narrative text, the implied reader is linked to the way in which this overall textual strategy is revealed sentence by sentence and paragraph by paragraph in the text. Hopefully, this distinction will become clear in the discussion in the rest of this chapter.

It is also necessary to remind you of another very important aspect. In the first chapter I introduced the notion *ideological perspective*. I used this concept to indicate the *evaluative* perspective in Biblical narratives. It is vital to realize that, generally, the purpose of Biblical narratives is not merely to convey information, to display certain narratological skills or to be examples of poetic beauty. Usually, the purpose is to *convince* the reader of a certain evaluative aspect. Thus, when we attempt to integrate the results of the analysis of various narratological aspects in terms of the relation between the implied author and the implied reader, we should keep in mind that the narrative strategy is dominated by the implied author's attempts to convey a certain ideological perspective to the implied reader.

In order to illustrate this process I shall discuss John 13:1-30: the Footwashing and the identification of the traitor.[1]

Introduction
[1]Now before the festival of the Passover, Jesus knew that his hour had come to depart from this world and go to the Father. Having loved his own who were in the world, he loved them to the end.

The Footwashing
[2]The devil had already put it into the heart of Judas son of Simon Iscariot to betray him. And during supper [3]Jesus, knowing that the Father had given all things into his hands, and that he had come from God and was going to God, [4]got up from the table, took off his outer robe, and tied a towel around himself. [5]Then he poured water into a basin and began to wash the disciples' feet and to wipe them with the towel that was tied around him.

First interpretation of the Footwashing
[6]He came to Simon Peter, who said to him, "Lord, are you going to wash my feet?" [7]Jesus answered, "You do not know now what I am doing, but later you will understand." [8]Peter said to him, "You will never wash my feet." Jesus answered, "Unless I wash you, you have no share with me." [9]Simon Peter said to him, "Lord, not my feet only but also my hands and my head!" [10]Jesus said to him, "One who has bathed does not need to wash, except for the feet, but is entirely clean. And you are clean, though not all of you." [11]For he knew who was to betray him; for this reason he said, "Not all of you are clean."

Second interpretation of the Footwashing
[12]After he had washed their feet, had put on his robe, and had returned to the table, he said to them, "Do you know what I have done to you? [13]You call me

Teacher and Lord - and you are right, for that is what I am. [14]So if I, your Lord and Teacher, have washed your feet, your also ought to wash one another's feet. [15]For I have set you an example, that you also should do as I have done to you. [16]Very truly, I tell you, servants are not greater than their master, nor are messengers greater than the one who sent them. [17]If you know these things, you are blessed if you do them.

Announcement of the betrayal
[18]I am not speaking of all of you; I know whom I have chosen. But it is to fulfill the scripture, 'The one who ate my bread has lifted his heel against me.' [19]I tell you this now, before it occurs, so that when it does occur, you may believe that I am he. [20]Very truly, I tell you, whoever receives one whom I send receives me; and whoever receives me receives him who sent me."

Exposure of the traitor
[21]<u>After saying this Jesus was troubled in spirit, and declared,</u> "Very truly, I tell you, one of you will betray me." [22]<u>The disciples looked at one another, uncertain of whom he was speaking.</u> [23]<u>One of his disciples - the one whom Jesus loved - was reclining next to him;</u> [24]<u>Simon Peter therefore motioned to him to ask Jesus of whom he was speaking.</u> [25]<u>So while reclining next to Jesus, he asked him,</u> "Lord, who is it?" [26]<u>Jesus answered,</u> "It is the one to whom I give this piece of bread when I have dipped it in the dish." <u>So when he had dipped the piece of bread, he gave it to Judas son of Simon Iscariot.</u> [27]<u>After he received the piece of bread, Satan entered into him. Jesus said to him,</u> "Do quickly what you are going to do." [28]<u>Now no one at the table knew why he said this to him.</u> [29]<u>Some thought that, because Judas had the common purse, Jesus was telling him,</u> "Buy what we need for the festival"; <u>or, that he should give something to the poor.</u> [30]<u>So, after receiving the piece of bread, he immediately went out. And it was night.</u>

The implied author in John 13:1-30

In line with the definition of the implied author provided above, I shall now discuss the overall textual organization of John 13:1-30. In order to achieve this, I shall first discuss all the individual narratological aspects in terms of the methodological guidelines discussed in Chapters 2-7 before outlining the textual strategy.

Narrator and narratee

In John 13:1-30 the implied author employs the narrator and the narratee in the following way:

With regard to temporal relations between the process of narration and the story that is narrated, it should be classified as an example of *ulterior narration*, since the story is narrated after the events have already taken place.

With regard to the narrative level, the type of narrator used by the implied author can be classified as follows:

* *Extradiegetic:* The narrator functions on the level of the "primary story" and is not embedded in the story itself.

* *Heterodiegetic*: The narrator is not linked to or identified as one of the characters in the story world, but tells the story in such a way that s/he functions as an on-looker.

* *Fairly perceptible:* There are clear signs of the narrator's presence in the text (underlined above). In the first 5 verses we hear the narrator's voice constantly. In verses 6-10 the narrator's presence is diminished due to the fact that the voices of two of the characters (Jesus and Peter) are heard. In these verses the narrator's presence is limited to introductory words. In verse 11 the narrator's presence can again be perceived due to an "aside" explaining Jesus' words in verse 10. In verses 12-30 the narrator's presence can also be classified as being fairly perceptible - in particular in verses 21-30. Its voice is heard in the following verses: the description of the setting (verse 12), some introductory words (verses 21a; 25a; 26a; 27b); the description of the disciples' reaction (verses 22-24; 28-29); the description of Jesus' act (verses 26b-27a) and the description of Judas's departure (verse 30).

* *Reliable*: Since there are no indications to the contrary, we can assume that the narrator is reliable.

* *Ideological function*: Basically the ideological perspective of the Fourth Gospel has to do with the identity of Jesus (that he is the Son of God) and humankind's reaction to his identity - either belief or rejection. (See, for example,

John 20:31.) This is stressed over and over again in the Gospel in one way or another. In this section the implied author uses the narrator to communicate this ideological perspective. For example, in verses 1-3 and 11 the implied author uses the narrator to draw attention to Jesus' foreknowledge - a trait characteristic of his unique identity.

Narratee: There are no clear signs of the presence of the narratee in this text and, accordingly s/he can be classified as being almost totally absent from the text. The only exception is the aside in verse 11 from which it can be inferred that the story is narrated to someone (the narratee) to whom Jesus' words in verse 10 ("And you are clean, though not all of you.") need to be explained. Furthermore, since there are no indications to the contrary we can classify the narratee as being on the same level as the narrator, that is *extradiegetic* and *heterodiegetic*.

Focalization

The implied author arranges the *locus of focalization* in such a way that it is situated externally. The events are portrayed in such a way that it seems as if they are "viewed" through the eyes of an onlooker who does not play any role in the story him/herself.

With regard to the *focalized objects* (the characters), we have several examples where they are focalized internally to some extent:

* Jesus is focalized internally in verses 1-3 (his foreknowledge and "love until the end" are indicated); verse 11 (his foreknowledge of the identity of the traitor is indicated) and verse 21 (his emotional distress is indicated).

* Judas Iscariot is focalized internally in verse 2 (The devil had already put it into his heart to betray Jesus.); as well as verse 27 (After he received the piece of bread, Satan entered into him.).

* The disciples are focalized internally in verse 29 as their thoughts are

portrayed.

It is important to note that, in each instance where the implied author uses internal focalization of the characters, this is done in order to communicate information that is vital in some way or another to grasping the ideological perspective of the Fourth Gospel. In the case of Jesus, this concerns his identity. In the case of Judas, it is necessary in order to link the act of betrayal to a much broader picture, namely the spiritual war between light and darkness. In the case of the disciples, it is used in order to indicate the poor way in which they follow Jesus - thereby serving as negative examples of discipleship.

Characters

In this section the following characters are portrayed: Jesus, the disciples (as a group), Peter, the Beloved Disciple, and Judas. They are characterized as follows:

> Jesus: Paradigm of traits
> - Complete knowledge
> - Love
> - Authority
> - Close relationship to the Father
> - Provides spiritual life

In this section Jesus' *complete knowledge* is indicated in several ways. In verse 1 the implied author uses the narrator to communicate the notion that Jesus knows that his hour has come to depart from the world (direct characterization). In verse 3 his complete knowledge is mentioned again (direct characterization). In verses 10 and 18-30 the same trait is illustrated by means of indirect characterization as Jesus reveals his knowledge of the betrayal and the identity of the traitor.

His *love* is indicated in several ways. In verse 1 the implied author uses the narrator to indicate the trait by means of direct characterization. In verses 3-11 the same trait is illustrated in the vivid portrayal of the act of the footwashing (indirect characterization).

His *authority* is illustrated in the way that he acts towards the disciples in this section, for example, by ordering them to follow his example, as well as the confident way in which he discusses future events (indirect characterization). In verse 14 the implied author uses Jesus himself to indicate this trait by means of direct characterization.

His *close relationship to the Father* is indicated by means of direct characterization in verse 3: the implied author uses the narrator to highlight this trait.

That he *provides spiritual life* becomes clear in the dialogue between him and Peter: Jesus answered: "Unless I wash you, you have no share with me." "To have share with Jesus" is a metaphorical way of expressing the idea that Jesus provides spiritual life.

In the case of the disciples (as a group) only one trait is highlighted in this section, namely that they are unable to understand Jesus. This is illustrated in Peter's reaction in verse 8, that can be seen as representative of that of all the disciples (indirect characterization). In verse 22 the implied author uses the narrator in order to indicate the same trait (indirect characterization). In verses 28-29 the disciples' (almost unbelievable!) reaction once again illustrates the same trait: even though Jesus identifies the traitor in a very clear way, they do not realize that it is Judas who will betray Jesus!

Another important aspect should be noted with regard to the characterization of the disciples: The implied author uses Jesus in order to indicate how the disciples *should* act, or, in other words, which traits they should have. In this regard the most important trait highlighted in this section is that they should be prepared to follow Jesus' example by serving one another in a loving way (see verse 15).

In this section certain individual disciples are characterized individually, too. *Peter* is characterized in terms of two traits, namely his impulsiveness (see his reaction in verses 8 and 9), and leadership (he acts as the spokesman of the group of disciples). In both cases this is achieved by means of indirect characterization.

The *Beloved Disciple* is characterized as having one (important) trait, namely that he is loved by Jesus (verse 23: direct characterization). This is also illustrated by means of indirect characterization, since he is portrayed as reclining next to Jesus.[2] In this way the implied author indicates that this disciple is to be viewed as the ideal disciple.

Judas Iscariot is mentioned several times. The implied author characterizes this character in terms of one trait only, namely the willingness of a follower of Jesus to betray him. This trait is linked directly to the Satan in verses 2 and 27 in such a way that Judas can be regarded as the embodiment of cosmic evil.

How should these characters *be classified*? If *E. M. Forster's* system is used, all the characters should be classified as flat, since none of them is really capable of surprising the implied reader (the criterion Forster indicates in order to determine whether characters are round or flat). If Forster's system is used in the adapted form (as I indicated in Chapter 4; pp. 54-55), Jesus could be classified as a round figure, since the paradigm of traits associated with him is larger than those associated with the other characters. If *Adele Berlin*'s system is used, Jesus should be classified as a full-fledged character whereas all the other characters (the disciples as a group, Peter, the Beloved Disciple and Judas) should be classified as types.

In terms of the system proposed by *W. J. Harvey*, Jesus should be classified as the protagonist and all the other characters as ficelles. In terms of *Joseph Ewen's* system, the characters can be classified as follows:

	Complexity	Development	Penetration into inner life
Jesus	Complex	None	A little
Disciples	Not complex	None	A little
Peter	Not complex	None	None
Beloved Disciple	Not complex	None	None
Judas	Not complex	None	A little

In terms of *Greimas's* actantial system, the constellation of characters in John 13:1-30 can be classified as follows:

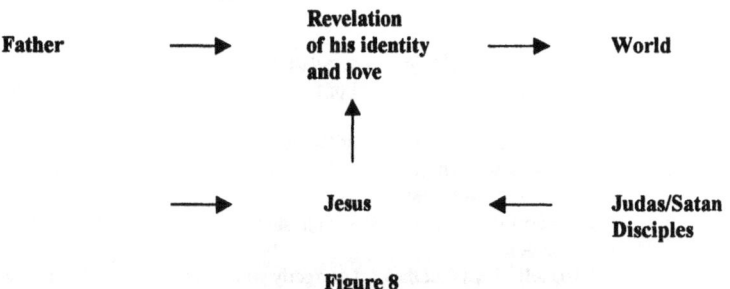

Figure 8

From all the classifications provided above it is clear that Jesus is portrayed as the central character in John 13:1-30.

Events

The surface structure of the events in John 13:1-30 will be discussed first. In the following diagram you will find the result of the following procedures:

a) A paraphrasing of the events
b) A classification of all the events
c) An indication of the kernels (underlined)
d) A summary of the microsequences (italics)

A: *Devil persuades Judas to betray Jesus.*
1. Devil puts it into Judas's heart to betray Jesus.   Mental act

B: *Jesus washes the feet of his disciples.*
1. Jesus gets up from the table.   Physical act
2. Jesus takes off his outer robe.   Physical act
3. Jesus ties a towel around himself.   Physical act
4. Jesus pours water into a basin.   Physical act
5. Jesus washes the disciples' feet.   Physical act

6.	Jesus wipes their feet with the towel.	Physical act
C:	*Jesus persuades Peter to let him wash his feet.*	
1.	Peter asks Jesus whether he is going to wash his feet.	Verbal act: Prohibition
2.	Jesus predicts that he will understand later.	Verbal act: Prediction
3.	Peter refuses to let him wash his feet.	Verbal act: Prohibition
4.	Jesus warns him against excluding himself from Jesus.	Verbal act: Warning
5.	Peter asks him to wash his feet, head and hands.	Verbal act: Request
6.	Jesus tells him that it is only necessary to wash his feet.	Verbal act: Advice
D:	*Jesus warns the disciples that not all of them are clean.*	
1.	Jesus warns them that not all of them are clean.	Verbal act: Warning
E:	*Jesus explains the meaning of the Footwashing.*	
1.	Jesus puts on his robe.	Physical act
2.	Jesus returns to the table.	Physical act
3.	Jesus asks them whether they understand what he has done.	Verbal act: Question
4.	Jesus tells them that they act correctly when they call him "Teacher and Lord".	Verbal act: Assertion
5.	Jesus commands them to follow his example.	Verbal act: Command
6.	Jesus promises them that they will be blessed if they obey him.	Verbal act: Promise
F:	*Jesus identifies the traitor.*	
1.	Jesus becomes troubled in spirit.	Emotional act
2.	Jesus announces that one of them will betray him.	Verbal act: Prediction
3.	The disciples look at one another.	Physical act
4.	Peter motions to the Beloved Disciple to ask Jesus of whom he is speaking.	Verbal act: Request
5.	Jesus answers that he will identify the traitor by giving him a piece of bread.	Verbal act: Promise
6.	Jesus gives the piece of bread to Judas.	Physical act
G:	*Satan enters Judas.*	
1.	Judas takes the piece of bread.	Physical act
2.	Satan enters Judas.	Mental act
H:	*Jesus urges Judas to carry out his plan.*	
1.	Jesus urges Judas to carry out his plan.	Verbal act: Command
2.	Some of the disciples think that Jesus is sending Judas out to buy what they need for the festival.	Mental act
3.	Some of the disciples think that Jesus is sending Judas to give something to the poor.	Mental act
4.	Judas goes out.	Physical act

The events indicated above are all *punctual* events. It should also be pointed out that the narrator mentions three others events in verses 1-3 that could be classified as *durative* events, namely Jesus' love for his own, his knowledge that his hour has come, and his knowledge of the traitor. These three events provide the reason for all the punctual events in John 13:1-30.

The overall picture is one of a sequence with a highly dramatic quality, as extraordinary physical events (such as the washing of the disciples' feet and the giving of the piece of bread) are mixed with a number of surprising verbal and other non-physical acts (such as the warning that not all of the disciples are clean and Satan entering Judas), reaching a climax with Judas's dramatic decision to leave the room and his disappearance into the night. However, it is important to note that the plot should be described as a process of improvement and not one of deterioration. The implied author makes it very clear that the events should not be interpreted as a catastrophe, since they happen according to God's plan.

With regard to the way in which the surface structure of events is organized, one can indicate several principles used by the implied author in order to combine the microsequences into a plot. The three most important principles that are used are chronology, causality and character. Chronology plays a role in the sense that the microsequences are organized in a chronological order. The principle of causality can be seen in the causal relationships that can be indicated between various microsequences, for example, A and G; B and C; C and E; D and F; and F and H. The principle of character can also be indicated, since one character (Jesus) dominates nearly all the microsequences. The other two principles, space and internal relationships, also play a role, but to a lesser extent. The principle of space is used in the sense that all the microsequences are situated within the same setting. The principle of internal relationships can be indicated in the case of microsequences A and C: in both cases a disciple is persuaded to do something.

In A the devil persuades Judas to betray Jesus and in C Jesus persuades Peter to have his feet washed.

Deep structure

In order to describe the deep structure of events in John 13:1-30, we have to uncover its underlying logic. As I indicated in Chapter 5, this is usually not expressed directly in the surface structure, and, accordingly, has to be reconstructed. To my mind the underlying logic of John 13:1-30 has to do with the *fundamental opposition between true and false discipleship*. This can be represented as follows in terms of a semiotic square:

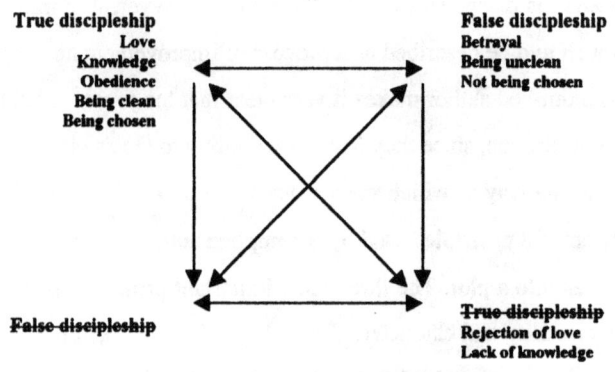

Figure 9

According to the logic of this semiotic square, humankind is faced with a fundamental choice, namely that of "true discipleship" *versus* "false discipleship". According to John 13:1-30, "true discipleship" is characterized by love, knowledge, obedience, being "clean" and being chosen.

In the case of the first component, *love*, this is expressed in verse 14. Significantly, this component is not only indicated as one of the requirements in order to qualify for "true discipleship", but is also associated with Jesus: in verse 1 his whole ministry is characterized in terms of love, and, furthermore, the footwashing itself is portrayed as a concrete expression of his love. In this way the implied author stresses the important function Jesus fulfills in constituting discipleship.

The second component, *knowledge*, is expressed in various ways: in verses 12 and 17 it is indicated as characteristic of the behavior expected from those who opt for "true discipleship". Furthermore, as in the case of the previous component, it is also stressed that knowledge is characteristic of Jesus himself. See verses 1, 2 and 11.

The third component, *obedience*, dominates the second interpretation of the Footwashing (verses 12-17), since Jesus' action is interpreted as an example to be followed by all those striving towards "true discipleship". See verses 14-15. Note that, once again, this component is also linked to Jesus himself: in verse 1 it is made clear that Jesus' actions are motivated by his knowledge that he has to return to the Father - thus an act of obedience.

The fourth component, *being clean*, is expressed in verses 10-11. This is meant in a spiritual sense. The fifth component, *being chosen*, is expressed in Jesus' words in verse 18: "I know whom I have chosen".

"True discipleship" is opposed by its contrary "False discipleship", thereby constituting an either ... or relationship between these two choices. "False discipleship" is represented in the text by the character Judas whose decision to betray Jesus is viewed extremely negatively. Whereas the components associated with "true discipleship" are linked to Jesus, Judas's decision is linked directly to Satan (see verses 2 and 27). In this way the opposition between "true discipleship" and "false discipleship" is depicted within a deeper dimension so characteristic of the Fourth Gospel, namely the opposition spiritual light *versus* spiritual darkness. Apart from the component "betrayal", two other components associated with "false discipleship" are also expressed in the text, namely being unclean in a spiritual sense (verses 10-11) and not being chosen (verse 18).

The third possibility on the semiotic square, namely that of the negation of "true discipleship" by "~~true discipleship~~" is represented in the narrative by the behavior of the disciples. Two components are indicated: firstly, *rejection of love* is expressed in Peter's unwillingness to have his feet washed by Jesus - an action that represents an unwillingness to accept Jesus' loving kindness.

Secondly, a *lack of knowledge* is evident throughout the narrative: Peter's decision not to have his feet washed by Jesus, is based on his lack of knowledge and understanding. A lack of knowledge is also depicted clearly in the way in which the disciples react to Jesus' announcement of the betrayal (see verse 22ff.). Even after the identification of Judas as the traitor, they remain ignorant.

According to the logic of the semiotic square, "false discipleship" implies "~~true discipleship~~". Thus, Judas, who embodies "false discipleship" should also give expression to the components associated with "~~true discipleship~~". This can be seen in the narrative in Judas's decision to leave the room after Jesus gives him the piece of bread (in those times regarded as a gesture of affection and honor). By this action Judas expresses *rejection of love* (the first component associated with ~~true discipleship~~). It seems strange that Judas has no objection against having his feet washed by Jesus, since this constitutes an acceptance of Jesus' love. In the surface structure of the text this comes to the fore in Jesus' statement in verse 10: "And you are clean, though not all of you." Although Judas's feet have been washed, this act has no effect on him, because he rejects this love by his decision to betray Jesus.

Interestingly enough, it should be noted that the possibility of "~~false discipleship~~" is not expressed in the narrative. The obvious reason for this is the statement in verse 18 ("But it is to fulfill the scripture, The one who ate my bread has lifted his heel against me.") - a statement that leaves no room for the negation of "false discipleship" by Judas, the character who embodies this value.

Time

With regard to *order*, only one example of anachrony in the true sense of the word can be indicated: in verse 2 the implied author uses an analepsis to indicate that the devil had already put it into Judas's heart to betray Jesus. This event happened earlier in the narrative, but is only narrated now. The reason for narrating this event now, and not earlier on in the narrative, seems to be that by placing it directly after verse 1, the implied author succeeds in conveying the broader framework within which the events that follow are to be narrated (God *versus* Satan, or spiritual *versus* the forces of darkness) very effectively.

It should also be noted that the implied author employs a number of embedded prolepses and analepses. For an embedded analepsis, see verses 3a, and for embedded prolepses, see verses 7, 11 and 18-20.

If this narrative is analyzed in terms of the way in which the implied author handles the aspect of *duration*, it should be pointed out that the technique used most often is that of *scenic representation*. The only exceptions are verses 1-2 (summary), as well as verses 11 and 23 (in both cases narrative pauses are used). The dominance of scenic representation enables the implied author to portray the events very vividly.

In terms of *frequency*, this narrative is an example of singulative frequency: events that happened once are narrated once. However, two significant exceptions should be noted: verse 1 represents an iterative summary, since the narrator is used to summarize and interpret all Jesus' actions in terms of his love for his own. This serves an important function in conveying the ideological perspective in this narrative. Secondly, an iterative summary is also used in verse 3: the implied author uses the narrator to summarize Jesus' knowledge of his authority, his origin and destination by means of a short statement. Once again, the function of this device is to draw attention to the ideological perspective of the narrative.

Setting

The implied author uses the setting in a very effective way. In verse 1 the narrator is used in order to provide a *chronological setting* ("before the festival of the Passover"). However, it is important to realize that this is much more than a mere indication of the chronological setting. Since Jesus has already been identified as the Lamb of God (see John 1:51), it is clear that this setting is very significant: his death will coincide with the Passover.

In verse 2 the implied author provides a *spatial setting*: the events that are to be narrated occur "during supper". This suggests an intimate setting: Jesus and his disciples are portrayed as reclining at a table somewhere *inside*, while it is getting dark *outside*.

The effective way in which the implied author uses verse 30 should also be noted: Judas is depicted as going outside, thus leaving the "inside" where Jesus is in order to go out into the darkness. Clearly this is not meant only as a spatial indication, but carries a symbolic meaning: Judas's movement into the darkness is indicative of the fact that he has fallen prey to the forces of darkness.

The implied author's textual strategy

From what I have discussed so far, it is clear that the main purpose of the implied author is to convey an ideological perspective to the implied reader. In order to achieve this purpose, the textual strategy is dominated by various attempts to convey this perspective. Of these the following are the most important:

* The implied author uses the narrator to emphasize Jesus' foreknowledge of future events and his love for his own by means of narrative pauses. These aspects are vital in order to grasp Jesus' identity.

* The surface structure of events is organized in such a way that the plot can be depicted as a series of improvement, thereby communicating the notion that the events should not be seen as a catastrophe befalling Jesus, but, instead, as happening according to a divine plan.

* The deep structure of events is organized in such a way that a powerful message is conveyed: humankind has to make a choice between true and false discipleship.

* The characters are portrayed in such a way that Jesus is presented as the dominating character. Several traits associated with him are indicated over and over again in such a way that his unique identity cannot be missed. The other characters are arranged in such a way that they represent various responses to Jesus' identity: Judas represents false discipleship since he has decided to betray Jesus and in this way has rejected his love. The Beloved Disciple represents the ideal disciple striving towards the ideal of true discipleship. The other disciples (including Peter) represent those disciples who are willing to follow Jesus (thus forming a category quite distinct from Judas), but unable to do it in the correct way.

* Both the chronological and spatial setting are used to reinforce the ideological perspective. The chronological setting ("before the Passover") links the coming events to Jesus' being the "Lamb of God". The spatial setting, in particular the contrast between "inside" and "darkness outside", is used in order to symbolize the (unsuccessful) onslaughts of the powers of darkness.

The interaction between implied author and implied reader in John 13:1-30

At this stage it may be necessary to remind you again of the difference between the implied author and the implied reader. Whereas I defined the implied author in terms of the overall textual organization of the narrative, I associated the implied reader with the *temporality* of the text. Thus, although the implied reader is also defined in terms of the way in which the narrative text is organized, the focus of our attention will not be the overall structure as such, but the way in which this overall structure is revealed to the reader verse by verse. To put it simply: when we discuss the implied reader, we investigate the way in which the narrative would have been read by someone reading it for the first time in the way the implied author intended it to be read. This interaction between implied author and implied reader in John 13:1-30 will now be discussed.

In this case we have to keep in mind that the implied reader has already read the first twelve chapters of the Fourth Gospel at this stage. Therefore it will be necessary to summarize shortly what has already been achieved in terms of the interaction between implied author and implied reader:

* The implied reader has already achieved a firm hold on the plot of the Fourth Gospel. It has come to understand that the plot of the Fourth Gospel basically focuses on the identity of Jesus and humankind's reaction to it.

* The implied reader has become aware that the narrative is entering its final stage. For example, the decision to kill Jesus (John 11:46-53), his triumphant entry into Jerusalem (John 12:12-19) and the announcement that his hour has come (John 12:23-36) all serve as clear signs that the final stage in the development of the plot has been reached.

* The most important observation with regard to the interaction between implied author and implied reader in the first twelve chapters of the Gospel is that this process is dominated by an emphasis on the ideological perspective, namely that Jesus is to be considered the Son of God. The purpose of the interaction is not only to convince the implied reader to evaluate all the events from the same ideological perspective as that accepted by the implied author, but, in the final instance, to guide it deeper into believing that Jesus is the Son of God, since by believing in him, it becomes possible to receive and experience spiritual life.

Against this background the interaction in John 13:1-30 can now be discussed in more detail.

Verse 1: Introduction

In the last verses of John 12 the implied author made use of scenic representation in which Jesus' direct words were presented to the implied reader. In John 13:1 this changes: Instead of the scenic representation used in John 12:44-50, he now uses the narrator to give an interpretative summary of all the events which are to follow. The following three aspects are important:

Firstly, the implied author provides the implied reader with a *chronological setting* for the events that are to follow, namely that they occur before the festival of the Passover. The implied reader, who is aware of the fact that Jesus is going to die and that he was identified as the "Lamb of God" by John the Baptist (see John 1:35), will be able to understand the ideological significance of this chronological setting.

Secondly, the implied reader is informed that *Jesus' hour* has arrived. This information forms part of a pattern created by the implied author in the Fourth Gospel. On three previous occasions the implied reader was informed that Jesus' hour had not yet come (John 2:4; 7:30; 8:20) - thus creating an expectation of the importance of the hour of glorification which was still to come. In John 12:23 and 12:27 the implied reader was informed that the hour of glorification had indeed come. Now, shortly after John 12:23 and 12:27, the implied author informs the implied reader for the third time that Jesus' hour has come. Together with the reference to the Passover, this serves to stress the significance of the events which are to follow.

Thirdly, the implied reader is once again presented with an ideological perspective on *Jesus' identity*. By means of indirect characterization two traits of Jesus - of which the implied reader already has knowledge - are reiterated. The first trait is his foreknowledge of future events. This emphasizes his identity as the Son of God. The second trait is his love for his own - a love "until the end" and "to the limit". This love is presented to the implied reader as a durative event and in this way highlights one of the wonderful benefits of being one of Jesus' "own", namely that of being loved by Jesus in a truly divine way.

Thus, verse 1 serves as a very important indication to the implied reader as to how the events that follow have to be evaluated. Clearly, the implied author is guiding the implied reader to accept an ideological perspective that views the coming death of Jesus not as a catastrophe, but as an event that forms a necessary part of Jesus' return to the Father, and in fact will be used to glorify him, and to demonstrate his love for his own.

Verses 2-5: The act of footwashing

In verses 2-3 the implied author continues the interpretative summary that began in verse 1, thereby communicating several important notions to the implied reader:

Firstly, verse 2 provides the implied reader with a *spatial setting*: The events that are to be narrated take place at a meal. No further information is provided at this stage.

Secondly, by means of internal focalization of one of the characters, *Judas*, important information about his intention to betray Jesus is provided to the implied reader. The information that Judas will betray Jesus will come as no surprise to the implied reader, since it has already been informed of this in John 6:71 and 12:4. What is new, however, is the explicit link between Judas's decision and the devil. This link is meant to guide it to evaluate Judas's actions and the events during Jesus' hour from a much wider perspective, namely that of the struggle between darkness and light.

Thirdly, by providing this disturbing information directly after having reminded the implied reader of Jesus' love for his own, the implied author forcefully puts across the notion of the radical *difference between true and false discipleship*. Judas's reaction to Jesus' love is an act indicative of false discipleship. His decision to betray Jesus is completely illogical and reprehensible, but he acts in this way, because he is manipulated by the devil. In spite of the privilege he had of being in Jesus' presence, he decides to act in a way typical of false discipleship.

Fourthly, the implied author quickly *reassures* the implied reader in verse 3. Jesus is internally focalized and two traits already known to the implied reader are once again underlined: Jesus' foreknowledge of events, as well as his close relationship with the Father: he knows that the Father has given all things into his hands, that he has come from God and that he is going to God. This ideological perspective is repeated in order to make it clear that Jesus is in full control of the situation. In spite of the devil's attempts *via* Judas Iscariot, he remains in control of the situation.

In verses 4 and 5 the implied author changes the presentation from a summary by the narrator to *scenic representation*. For the first time since John 12:12-19 (Jesus' entry into Jerusalem), physical events are narrated. This is achieved in a very effective way. The implied author succeeds in portraying Jesus' actions vividly by narrating his actions step by step: Jesus gets up from the table, takes off his outer robe, takes a towel and ties it around himself, pours water into the basin and begins to wash the disciples' feet. This astonishing act will surprise the implied reader, since this task was usually performed by slaves. Nevertheless, having just been reminded in the narrator's summary of Jesus' love for his own, it will be able to understand this act of utmost humiliation as being indicative of Jesus' love. Being fully aware of Jesus' real identity, it will be able to comprehend fully the stark contrast between who Jesus really is and the position that he assumes.

On the basis of verses 2-5, the implied reader will also be able to gain a better picture of the *setting* of the events: The scene consists of Jesus and the disciples who are having a meal before the Passover. From the scenic representation of the Footwashing, the implied reader can also gather that, with the exception of the disciples, no other persons are present - thus, an intimate scene between Jesus and his disciples is portrayed.

Verses 6-11: First interpretation of the Footwashing

Nearly the whole section (verse 11 is the only exception) is presented by means of scenic representation. The primary function of this section is to guide the implied reader towards discovering the *significance of the Footwashing*. In verse 7 Jesus answers the objection raised by Peter as follows: "You do not know what I am doing, but later you will understand." This serves as an indication to the implied reader that the real significance of Jesus' act is linked to an important event lying in the future. In this regard verse 8b functions as the focal point: "Unless I wash you, you have no share with me." Thus, the implied author guides the implied reader to link three concepts: being washed by Jesus, having a share with him, and (a) future event(s). Since the only future events the implied reader has knowledge of at this stage concern the events of Jesus' hour, namely his departure/death/resurrection (see John 2:21-22; 3:14-15; 7:33-34 and 12:30-35), the only conclusion that it can reach is that the significance of the Footwashing lies in its reference to these events. In other words, it is guided to understand that the Footwashing should be interpreted as signifying the future events through which the disciples can "have a share with Jesus". Accordingly, as a result of the narration of the Footwashing, the implied reader is already in a position to gain two important insights with regard to Jesus' "departure": Firstly, it becomes clear that it is to be seen as an act of loving kindness. Secondly, it is indicated that these events are of vital importance for "having a share with Jesus" or, in other words, the implied author emphasizes the vital role that Jesus plays in constituting discipleship.

Although the implied author primarily uses this section to guide the implied reader towards understanding the significance of the Footwashing, the way in which this is done also sheds light on the characterization of two of the characters, namely Peter and Jesus. That *Peter* is the only disciple to raise an objection to the menial task performed by Jesus, confirms the implied reader's impression that Peter is to be seen as the leader/spokesman of the disciples (see John 6:68). In addition to this trait, the implied reader is also guided to perceive a new trait to be associated with this character: By means of his words in verse 8, "You will never wash my feet!" (indirect characterization), the implied author illustrates the trait of impulsiveness in Peter. This is also illustrated in verse 9: "Lord, not my feet only but also my hands and my head!"

With regard to *Jesus*, the way in which he acts in this scene confirms the implied reader's knowledge of a number of traits already associated with him - especially his authoritative behavior and the fact that he can provide spiritual life. Furthermore, Jesus' success in persuading Peter to accept the symbolic washing of his feet, is narrated as an act parallel to the devil's persuasion of Judas (verse

2). Jesus' success in persuading Peter reminds the implied reader of the devil's success in persuading Judas - two parallel acts portraying two totally opposite ways of behavior possible for mankind.

In verse 11 the implied author introduces a narrative pause and then makes use of internal focalization to direct the implied reader's attention once again to Jesus' foreknowledge of events - in this case, his foreknowledge of the betrayal and the identity of the traitor. By emphasizing this ability of Jesus, as well as the fact that he enters his hour fully aware of everything that will happen to him, the implied reader is again reminded of the ideological perspective on the identity of Jesus. This narrative pause is introduced by the implied author in order to explain Jesus' statement that not all of the disciples are clean. By means of the contrast clean/not clean, the implied author also focuses the implied reader's attention on one of the differences between true discipleship/false discipleship.

Verses 12-17: Second interpretation of the Footwashing

In this section the implied author confronts the implied reader with some of the *demands* inherent in discipleship. In other words, it shows the implied reader that being a disciple does not only imply having certain things done for one by Jesus, but also entails having to do certain things oneself. Two aspects are important in this regard, namely the content of, and the motivation for the demand.

With regard to the first aspect, the *content* of the command, this is worded in verse 14 as a command that the disciples should wash one another's feet. The implied reader who, in the previous section has been led to grasp the symbolic nature of Jesus' act of footwashing, namely as referring to (a) future event(s) whereby Jesus lovingly makes it possible for his "own" to "have a share with him", will understand that the command requires much more from disciples than a mere physical washing of one another's feet. It is not physical washing of feet that is required by Jesus, but a way of living similar to that which Jesus has just demonstrated. Without even having mentioned the word, the implied author has made the demand crystal clear to the implied reader: Love!

With regard to the second aspect, namely the *motivation* for this command, it is important to note that, before Jesus gives the command, the narrator tells how Jesus puts his clothes back on and returns to his place at the table. The slave has once again become the master! And as master Jesus can give the command: "If I ... then you ought!" The contrast between Jesus' position and that of the disciples is repeated several times (verses 13, 14 and 16). In this way the motivation for the command is made perfectly clear to the implied reader: Discipleship implies obedience. If the master commands, the slaves should obey. However, there is more to it. The slaves are not expected to obey only because the master commands them to do so, but also because the master has already set the example of what to do and how it is to be done.

The fact that the previous section already contained an interpretation of the Footwashing, means that the implied reader will have to decide on the relationship between the two interpretations. Since the two interpretations do not stand in contrast to one another, the implied reader will be able to integrate them. The most obvious way in which this can be achieved is by means of a causal relationship: Since Jesus' role is crucial in constituting discipleship, his example should be followed.

Verses 18-20: Announcement of the betrayal

With regard to the interaction between implied author and implied reader in this section, the following two aspects are important:

Firstly, after the strong emphasis on the positive way in which discipleship should be manifested, the implied author once again introduces the *contrast* between true and false discipleship. This is achieved as follows: Jesus reminds the disciples that what he said to them, does not apply to all of them, since, even within this intimate group sharing a meal with him, there is someone who does not really belong there. Not all of them will be able to follow his example; indeed, someone close to him will lift his heel against him (verse 18). It is important to note how the implied author organizes this scene. Although the announcement of the betrayal is the focal point, it is placed within a context that is dominated by reassurances that Jesus is, nevertheless, in control of the situation. In verse 18 it is made clear that the traitor will be fulfilling the Scripture - thus the betrayal forms part of a divine plan and will not take the Father and Jesus by surprise. Furthermore, although the betrayal will be a deplorable act, it will have a positive effect in the sense that it will strengthen the disciples' belief in Jesus (verse 19), since, when they look back to this evening, the fact that he was able to make this prediction in advance, will serve as a confirmation of his identity: "... so that ... you may believe that I am he" - that is, the Son of God. The reassuring nature of this section can also be seen in the way in which true discipleship and false discipleship are contrasted. Whereas false discipleship is associated with the deplorable act of lifting one's heel against the one with whom you are eating bread, true discipleship is associated with the reassuring knowledge of being chosen (verse 18).

Secondly, it should be noted how the implied author succeeds in *creating suspense* in this scene. The implied reader has already been informed of the betrayal and the identity of the traitor, but at this stage the disciples do not know anything about Judas's intention. The implied author has also indicated that events are drawing to a close. Furthermore, he has twice in this chapter reminded the implied reader of Judas's intention to betray Jesus (verses 2 and 10-11). At this stage Jesus' words make sense to the implied reader, since at this stage it has more knowledge than the disciples. The disciples, however, are not yet able to grasp the meaning of his words. Thus, the implied reader is forced to ask the question, "Is Jesus going to reveal his foreknowledge of the betrayal and the identity of the traitor to the disciples? And if so, what will Judas's reaction be?".

Verses 21-30: The exposure of the traitor (John 13:21-30)

The implied reader does not have to wait long to discover whether Jesus is going to reveal his knowledge of the betrayal and the identity of the traitor explicitly to the disciples. In verse 21 Jesus reveals that one of them will betray him. This announcement is received in shocked silence. The implied author draws the implied reader's attention to Jesus' emotional behavior while making the announcement ("Jesus was troubled in spirit") - something that is noteworthy, since this is one of the few examples in the Fourth Gospel where Jesus is portrayed as demonstrating some kind of emotional behavior. In this case his "troubling of spirit" is caused by the grave announcement he has to make. In this way the implied reader is brought under the impression of the deplorable nature of Judas's intended act. The contrast between the nature of true and false discipleship is thus conveyed vividly to him/her.

In verse 23 the implied author introduces a new character, the *Beloved Disciple*, for the first time in the Gospel. Note that the implied reader is surprised by the revelation of this character at exactly the same moment that the disciples are wondering which of them will betray Jesus. Furthermore, it is also important to note that the implied author conveys two important notions with regard to the Beloved Disciple to the implied reader: Firstly, the description in verse 23 makes it very clear that this disciple is exceptionally close to Jesus: Not only is he described as the disciple "whom Jesus loved", but he reclines "next to Jesus".

Secondly, Peter's reaction in verse 24 (he does not ask Jesus himself, but motions to the Beloved Disciple to ask Jesus) serves as an indication to the implied reader that even Peter (whom the implied reader has been guided to accept as the leader of the disciples) regards this disciple as being closer to Jesus than himself. Thus the way in which the implied author introduces this character serves as an indication to the implied reader to view this disciple as Jesus' best follower amongst the disciples.

In verses 25-27 the implied author portrays Jesus' identification of the traitor by means of scenic representation. By this act - the first physical act narrated since the Footwashing - Jesus achieves three things: Firstly, he identifies the disciple of whom he has been talking. Secondly, he indicates to Judas that he knows of his intention to betray him. Thirdly, by giving him a piece of bread (an act considered to be a gesture of hospitality and affection), he is reaching out to him in love for the last time.

In verse 27 Judas makes the final decision. In spite of all the love he has received from Jesus, he still decides to betray him. The internal focalization in this verse is used by the implied author in a highly effective way to indicate to the implied reader how Judas reacts when he realizes that Jesus knows of his intention: There is no regret or change of mind, but, instead he is completely overmastered by Satan who is about to use him in the struggle against the light. Jesus, who is in full control of the events, does not try to prevent him. On the contrary, he urges Judas to carry out his plan. Thus, once again the implied author organizes the narrative in such a way that the ideological perspective dominates the communication process: The notions of Jesus' identity on the one hand (especially, his authoritative behavior, love and complete knowledge) and the reprehensible nature of false discipleship on the other hand are contrasted.

In verses 22 and 28-29 the implied reader's attention is drawn to the reaction of the disciples. It is clear that Jesus' announcement comes as a complete shock to them. Contrary to what might reasonably be expected, the disciples do not even understand the clear identification of the traitor. By means of internal focalization the implied reader is given access to the inner thoughts of the disciples (verses 28-29), making it quite clear that they do not understand: They are under the impression that Jesus is sending Judas to buy what is needed for the Festival, or to give something to the poor. Their reaction fits the paradigm of traits that the implied reader has constructed thus far in relation to this group of characters - especially with regard to their *inability to understand Jesus*.

Verse 27b ("Do quickly what you are going to do!") serves as an indication to the implied reader that the *final sequence* of events cannot be far off. Significantly, this process is not initiated by Satan or the world, but by Jesus himself. By identifying Judas as the traitor and by ordering him to proceed, Jesus initiates the last series of events that will end in his death and resurrection. This ideological perspective is conveyed in order to remind the implied reader, once again, that Jesus' death is not to be viewed as a catastrophe that befell him, but that everything that is about to happen to him forms part of his mission to the world.

The words "It was night" in verse 30 have *symbolic overtones*. The implied reader will understand that these words imply much more than a mere indication that it was physically dark outside. That Judas moves out of this space ("outside"), focalized as an intimate situation between Jesus and the disciples, into the dark night ("outside") serves as a symbolic indication of the implication of his decision: He has become part of the forces of darkness. In this way the implied author once again underlines the ideological perspective whereby a radical distinction is made between being part of the world and discipleship - a distinction that is linked to and reflects the radical difference between the forces of light and darkness.

Notes

[1] This discussion is based on my research on John 13:1-17:26. For a more technical and detailed analysis of this section, as well as the other four chapters, see my *Jesus' Farewell*.

[2] In the Greek text the words that are used ("in the bosom of Jesus") recall John 1:18, where Jesus' relationship to the Father is described in the same way.

BIBLIOGRAPHY

Alter, Robert, & Kermode, Frank. *The Literary Guide to the Bible*. Cambridge: Belknap Press, 1987.
Alter, Robert. *The Art of Biblical Narrative*. New York: Basic Books, 1981.
Alter, Robert. *The World of Biblical Literature*. New York: Basic Books, 1992.
Amit, Yairah. "'The Glory of Israel Does Not Deceive Or Change His Mind': On the Reliability of Narrator and Speakers in Biblical Narrative", *Prooftexts* 12 (1992): 201-212.
Auerbach, Erich. *Mimesis. Dargestellte Wirklichkeit in der abendländischen Literatur*. Bern: Francke, 1946. English translation by Willard Trask. Garden City: Doubleday, 1957.
Bal, Mieke. "The Laughing Mice, or: On Focalisation", *Poetics Today* 2/2 (1981): 202-210.
Bal, Mieke. *Lethal Love. Feminist Literary Readings of Biblical Love Stories*. Bloomington: Indiana University Press, 1987.
Bal, Mieke. *Narratology. Introduction to the Theory of Narrative*. Toronto: University of Toronto Press, 1985
Barat, Karen A. "Mission in Matthew. The Second Discourse as Narrative", in *SBL 1988 Seminar Papers*, ed. David J. Lull, (Atlanta: Scholars, 1988), 527-535.
Bar-Efrat, Shimon. *Narrative Art in the Bible*. Sheffield: Almond, 1989.
Barthes, Roland. *The Semiotic Challenge*. New York: Hill & Wang, 1988.
Beardslee, William A. *Literary Criticism of the New Testament*. Philadelphia: Fortress Press, 1970.
Beekman, K. D. & Fontijn, J. "Roman-figuren I", *Spektator* 1 (1971): 406-413.
Berendsen, Marjet. "The Teller and the Observer: Narration and Focalization in Narrative Texts", *Style* 18/2 (1984): 140-159.
Berlin, Adele. "Characterization in Biblical Narrative: David's Wives", *JSOT* 23 (1982): 69-85.
Berlin, Adele. *Poetics and Interpretation of Biblical Narrative*. Sheffield: Almond, 1983.
Black, C. Clifton III. "Depth of Characterisation and Degrees of Faith in Matthew", in *1989 SBL Seminar Papers*, ed. David J. Lull, (Atlanta: Scholars Press, 1989), 604-623.
Boers, Hendrikus. *Neither on This Mountain Nor in Jerusalem. A Study of John 4*. Atlanta: Scholars Press, 1988.
Boomershine, Thomas & Bartholomew, Gilbert. "Narrative Technique of Mark 16:8", *JBL* 100 (1981): 213-223.
Booth, Wayne C. *The Rhetoric of Fiction*. Chicago: Chicago University Press, 1961/1983.
Boulton, Marjorie. *The Anatomy of the Novel*. London: Routledge & Kegan Paul, 1975.

Brenner, Athalya. "Job the Pious? The Character of Job in the Narrative Framework of the Book", *JSOT* 43 (1989): 37-52.
Brink, André P. *Vertelkunde. 'n Inleiding tot die Lees van Verhalende Tekste*. Pretoria: Academica, 1987.
Brooks, Cleanth & Warren, Robert Penn. *Understanding Fiction*. New York: Appleton-Century-Crofts, 1943.
Brooks, Peter. *Reading for Plot. Design and Intention in Narrative*. Oxford: Clarendon, 1984.
Brown, Raymond E. *The Gospel According to John. Volume 2: John 13-21*. London: Geoffrey Chapman, 1966.
Campbell, Edward J. *Ruth. A New Translation with Introduction, Notes and Commentary*. New York: Doubleday, 1975.
Carter, Warren. "Kernels and Narrative Blocks in Matthew", *CBQ* 54/3 (1992): 463-481.
Caserio, Robert L. *Plot, Story and the Novel From Dickens and Poe to the Modern Period*. Princeton: Princeton University Press, 1979.
Caspi, Michael Maswari. "The Story of the Rape of Dinah: The Narrator and the Reader", *HebStud* 26/1 (1985): 25-45.
Chatman, Seymour. "On the Formalist-Structuralist Theory of Character", *Journal of Literary Semantics* 1 (1972): 57-79.
Chatman, Seymour. *Story and Discourse. Narrative Structure in Fiction and Film*. Ithaca: Cornell University Press, 1978.
Cixous, Helene. "The Character of 'Character'", *New Literary History* 5 (1974): 383-402.
Claassens, L. M. J. "Notes on Characterisation in the Jephtah Narrative", *Journal of North West Semitic Languages* 22/2 (1996): 107-115.
Clines, David J. A., Gunn, David M. & Hauser, Alan J. Eds. *Art and Meaning. Rhetoric in Biblical Literature*. Sheffield: JSOT Press, 1982.
Cohan, Steven & Shires, Linda M. *Telling Stories. A Theoretical Analysis of Narrative Fiction*. New York: Routledge, 1988.
Cohn, Robert L. *The Shape of Sacred Space: Four Biblical Studies*. Chico: Scholars Press, 1981.
Cooper, Alan. "Narrative Theory and the Book of Job", *SR* 11 (1982): 35-44.
Craig, Kenneth M. *A Poetics of Jonah*. Columbia: University of South Columbia, 1993.
Creech, R. Robert. "The Most Excellent Narratee: The Significance of Theophilus in Luke-Acts", in *With Steadfast Purpose. Essays on Acts in Honor of Henry Jackson Flanders, Jr.*, ed. Naymond H. Keathley, (Waco: Baylor University Press, 1990), 107-127.
Crittenden, Charles. "Fictional Characters and Logical Completeness", *Poetics* 11 (1982): 331-344.
Culley, Robert C. *Themes and Variations. A Study of Action in Biblical Narrative*. Atlanta: Scholars Press, 1997.
Culpepper, R. Alan. *Anatomy of the Fourth Gospel. A Study in Literary Design*. Philadelphia: Fortress, 1983.
Danove, Paul. "The Characterization and Narrative Function of the Women at the Tomb (Mark 15,40-41.47; 16,1-8)", *Bib* 77/3 (1996): 375-397.
Darr, John A. *Paradigms of Perception: The Reader and the Characters of Luke-Acts*. Louisville: Westminster, 1992.
Dawsey, James M. *The Lukan Voice. Confusion and Irony in the Gospel of Luke*. Macon: Mercer University Press, 1986.
Day, Linda. *Three Faces of a Queen. Characterization in the Books of Esther*. Sheffield: Sheffield Academic Press, 1995.
Deist, Ferdinand E. "A Note on the Narrator's Voice in Genesis 37, 20-22," *ZAW* 108/4 (1996): 621-622.

Deist, Ferdinand E. & Vorster, Willem S. Eds. Words from Afar: The Literature of the Old Testament. Volume 1. Cape Town: Tafelberg, 1989.
Dembinski, Jos. "Focalization and the First Person Narrator: A Revision of Theory", Poetics Today 10/4 (1989): 730-735.
Eco, Umberto. The Role of the Reader. Explorations in the Semiotics of the Text. London: Hutchinson, 1979.
Edminston, William F. "Focalizaton and the First-Person Narrator: A Revision of Theory", Poetics Today 10/4 (1989): 729-743.
Edwards, O. C. Luke's Story of Jesus. Philadelphia: Fortress, 1981.
Edwards, Richard A. Matthew's Story of Jesus. Philadelphia: Fortress, 1985.
Eslinger, Lyle. Into the Hands of the Living God. Sheffield: Almond Press, 1980.
Ewen, Joseph. "The Theory of Character in Narrative Fiction", Hasifrut 3 (1974): 1-30.
Ferraro, Fernando. "Theory and Model for the Structural Analysis of Fiction", New Literary History 5 (1974): 245-268.
Fewell, Danna Nolan & Gunn, David Miller. Compromising Redemption. Relating Characters in the Book of Ruth. Louisville: Westminster, John Knox, 1990.
Fields, Weston F. Sodom and Gomorrah. History and Motif in Biblical Narrative. Sheffield: Sheffield Academic Press, 1997.
Fokkelman, Jan P. Narrative Art and Poetry in the Books of Samuel. Volume 1: King David. Full Interpretation Based on Stylistic and Structural Analyses. Assen: Van Gorcum, 1981.
Forster, E. M. Aspects of the Novel. London: Edward Arnold, 1944.
Fowler, Robert M. "Who is the 'Reader' of Mark's Gospel?", SBL Seminar Papers 1983, ed. Kent Harold Richards, (Chico: Scholars Press, 1983), 31-53.
Fowler, Robert M. Let the Reader Understand. Reader-Response Criticism and the Gospel of Mark. Minneapolis: Fortress, 1991.
Fowler, Roger. "How to See Through Language: Perspective in Fiction", Poetics 11 (1982): 213-235.
Friedman, Norman. "Point of View in Fiction: The Development of a Critical Concept", PMLA 70 (1955): 1160-1184.
Frye, Northrop. Anatomy of Criticism. Four Essays. Princeton: Princeton University Press, 1957.
Frye, Northrop. The Great Code: The Bible and Literature. New York: Harcourt Brace Jovanovich, 1982.
Funk, Robert W. The Poetics of Biblical Narrative. Sonoma: Polebridge, 1988.
Garvey, James. "Characterisation in Narrative", Poetics 7 (1978): 63-78.
Genette, Gérard. Narrative Discourse Revisited. Translated from the French by Jane E. Lewin. Ithaca: Cornell University Press, 1988.
Genette, Gérard. Narrative Discourse. Translated from the French by Jane E. Lewin. Oxford: Basil Blackwell, 1980.
Gowler, David B. Host, Guest, Enemy and Friend: Portraits of the Pharisees in Luke and Acts. New York: Peter Lang, 1991.
Green, Barbara. "The Determination of Pharaoh: His Characterization in the Joseph Story (Genesis 37-50), in The World of Genesis. Persons, Places, Perspectives, eds. Philip R. Davies & David J. A. Clines (Sheffield: Sheffield Academic Press, 1998), 150-171.
Green, Barbara. "The Plot of the Biblical Story of Ruth", JSOT 23 (1982): 55-68.
Greimas, A. J. "Elements of a Narrative Grammar", Diacritics 7 (1977): 23-40;
Greimas, A. J. Sémantique structurale. Recherche dé méthode. Paris: Librairie Larousse, 1966.
Greimas, A. J. & Courtés, J. Semiotics and Language. An Analytical Dictionary. Bloomington: Indiana University Press, 1982.
Gunkel, Herman. Genesis. Göttingen: Vandenhoeck & Ruprecht, 1977. First published 1901.

Gunn, David M. "Reading Right. Reliable and Omniscient Narrator, Omniscient God, and Foolproof Composition in the Hebrew Bible", in *The Bible in Three Dimensions. Essays in Celebration of Forty Years of Biblical Studies in the University of Sheffield*, eds. David J. A. Clines, Stephen E. Fowl, & Stanley E. Porter, (Sheffield: Sheffield Academic Press, 1990), 53-64.

Gunn, David M. "The 'Hardening of the Pharaoh's Heart': Plot, Character and Theology in Exodus 1-14", in *Art and Meaning: Rhetoric in Biblical Literature*, eds. David J. A. Clines, David M. Gunn, & Alan J. Hauser, (Sheffield: JSOT, 1982), 72-96.

Gunn, David M. & Fewell, Danna Nolan. *Narrative in the Hebrew Bible*. Oxford: Oxford University Press, 1993.

Haenchen, Ernst. *The Acts of the Apostles*. Oxford: Basil Blackwell, 1971.

Hallberg, Calinda Ellen. "Storyline and Theme in Biblical Narrative: 1 Samuel 3", *OPTAT: Occasional Papers in Translation and Text Linguistics* 3 (1989): 1-35.

Harvey, W. J. *Character and the Novel*. London: Chatto & Windus, 1965.

Hauser, Alan John. "Genesis 2-3: The Theme of Intimacy and Alienation", in *Art and Meaning: Rhetoric in Biblical Literature*, eds. David J. A. Clines, David M. Gunn, & Alan J. Hauser, (Sheffield: JSOT Press, 1982), 20-36.

Hawk, L. Daniel. *Every Promise Fulfilled. Contesting Plots in Joshua*. Louisville: Westminster, John Knox, 1991.

Hedrick, Charles W. "Narrator and Story in the Gospel of Mark: Hermeneia and Paradosis", *PRSt* 14 (1987): 239-258.

Herman, David. "Hypothetical Focalization", *Narrative* 2/3 (1994): 230-253.

Hochman, Baruch. *Character in Literature*. Ithaca: Cornell, 1985.

Holleran, J. Warren. "Seeing the Light. A Narrative Reading of John 9", *EThL* 69 (1993): 5-26 and 354-382.

Howell, David B. *Matthew's Inclusive Story. A Study in the Narrative Rhetoric of the First Gospel*. Sheffield: JSOT Press, 1990.

Hubbard, Robert L. *The Book of Ruth*. Grand Rapids: Eerdmans, 1988.

Humphreys, W. Lee. *Joseph and his Family. A Literary Study*. Columbia: University of South Carolina Press, 1988.

Iser, Wolfgang. *The Act of Reading: A Theory of Aesthetic Response*. Baltimore: Johns Hopkins University Press, 1978.

Iser, Wolfgang. *The Implied Reader: Patterns of Communication in Prose Fiction from Bunyan to Bennett*. Baltimore: Johns Hopkins University Press, 1978.

Jasper, Alison. "Interpretative Approaches to John 20:1-18: Mary at the Tomb of Jesus", *StTh* 47/2 (1993), 107-118.

Jeansonne, Sharon Pace. "The Character of Lot in Genesis", *BTB* 18 (1988): 123-129.

Jobling, David. *The Sense of Biblical Narrative. Structural Analysis of the Hebrew Bible*. Two volumes. Sheffield: JSOT, 1986.

Kanzog, Klaus. *Eine Einführung in die Normeinübing des Erzählens*. Heidelberg: Quelle & Meyer, 1976.

Kelber, Werner H. *Mark's Story of Jesus*. Philadelphia: Fortress, 1979.

Kenney, William. *How to Analyze Fiction*. New York: Monarch Press, 1966.

Kermode, Frank. *The Genesis of Secrecy: On the Interpretation of Narrative*. Cambridge: Harvard University Press, 1979.

Kingsbury, Jack Dean. "The Figure of Jesus in Matthew's Story: A Literary-Critical Probe", *JSNT* 21 (1984): 3-36.

Kingsbury, Jack Dean. "The Plot of Matthew", *Interp* 46/4 (1992): 347-356.

Kingsbury, Jack Dean. *Conflict in Luke: Jesus, Authorities, Disciples*. Minneapolis: Fortress, 1991.

Kingsbury, Jack Dean. *Conflict in Mark. Jesus, Authorities and Disciples.* Minneapolis: Fortress, 1989.
Kingsbury, Jack Dean. *Matthew as Story.* Philadelphia: Fortress, 1988.
Kisling, Paul J. *Reliable Characters in the Primary History. Profiles of Moses, Joshua, Elijah and Elisha.* Sheffield: Sheffield Academic Press, 1996.
Klauck, Hans-Josef. "Die erzählerische Rolle der Jünger im Markusevangelium. Eine narrative Analyse", *NT* 24/1 (1982): 1-26.
Knott, William C. *The Craft of Fiction.* Reston: Reston Publishing Company, 1977.
Kunin, Seth D. "The Bridegroom of Blood: A Structural Analysis," *JSOT* 70 (1996): 3-16.
Kurz, William S. "Effects of Variant Narrators in Acts 10-11", *NTS* 43 (1997): 570-586.
Kurz, William S. "Narrative Approaches to Luke-Acts", *Bib* 68 (1987): 195-220.
Kurz, William S. "Narrative Models for Imitation in Luke-Acts", in *Greeks, Romans, and Christians*, eds. David L. Balch, Everett Ferguson & Wayne A. Meeks, (Minneapolis: Fortress, 1990), 171-189.
Kurz, William S. *Reading Luke-Acts. Dynamics of Biblical Narrative.* Louisville: Westminster, John Knox, 1993.
Lambe, Anthony J. "Genesis 38: Structure and Literary Design", in *The World of Genesis. Persons, Places, Perspectives*, eds. Philip R. Davies & David J. A. Clines, (Sheffield: Sheffield Academic Press, 1998), 102-120.
Lategan, Bernard C. "Coming to Grips with the Reader", *Semeia* 48 (1989): 3-17.
Licht, Jacob. *Storytelling in the Bible.* Jerusalem: Magnes Press, 1978.
Longman, Tremper. *Literary Approaches to Biblical Interpretation.* Grand Rapids: Zondervan, 1987.
Lubbock, Percy. *The Craft of Fiction.* London: Garden City, 1921.
Macauley, Robie & Lanning, George. *Technique in Fiction.* New York: Harper & Row, 1964.
Maccoby, Hyam. *Judas Iscariot and the Myth of Jewish Evil.* New York: Free Press, 1992.
Malbon, Elizabeth Struthers & Berlin, Adele. Eds. Characterization in Biblical Literature. *Semeia* 63 (1993).
Malbon, Elizabeth Struthers. "Disciples/Crowds/Whoever: Markan Characters and Readers", *NT* 28 (1986): 104-130.
Malbon, Elizabeth Struthers. "The Jesus of Mark and the Sea of Galilee", *JBL* 103/3 (1984): 363-377.
Malbon, Elizabeth Struthers. "The Major Importance of Minor Characters in Mark", in *The New Literary Criticism and the New Testament*, eds. Elizabeth Struthers Malbon & Edgar V. Knight, (Sheffield: Sheffield Academic Press, 1994), 58-86.
Malbon, Elizabeth Struthers. *Narrative Space and Mythic Meaning in Mark.* San Francisco: Harper & Row, 1986.
Malina, Bruce J. & Rohrbaugh, Richard L. *Social Science Commentary on the Synoptic Gospels.* Minneapolis: Fortress, 1992.
Martin, Wallace. *Recent Theories of Narrative.* Ithaca: Cornell, 1986.
Matera, Frank J. "The Plot of Matthew's Gospel", *CBQ* 49 (1987): 233-253.
McConville, J. G. & Millar, J. G. *Time and Place in Deuteronomy.* Sheffield: Sheffield Academic Press, 1994.
McKnight, Edgar. *The Bible and the Reader. An Introduction to Literary Criticism.* Philadelphia: Fortress, 1985.
Menn, Esther Marie. *Judah and Tamar (Genesis 38) in Ancient Jewish Exegesis. Studies in Literary Form and Hermeneutics.* Leiden: E J Brill, 1997.
Moloney, Francis J. "Who is 'the Reader' in/of the Fourth Gospel?", *ABR* 40 (1992): 20-33.
Moore, Stephen D. *Literary Criticism and the Gospels. The Theoretical Challenge.* New Haven: Yale University Press, 1989.

Mudrick, Marvin. "Character and Event in Fiction", *YR* 50 (1961): 202-218.
Nelles, William. "Getting Focalization into Focus", *Poetics Today* 11/2 (1990): 365-382.
Nicol, George G. "The Narrative Structure and Interpretation of Gen XXVI 1-31," *Vetus Testamentum* 96 (1996): 339-360.
Noegel, Scott B. "A Crux and a Taunt: Night Time Then Sunset in Genesis 15", in *The World of Genesis. Persons, Places, Perspectives,* eds. Philip R. Davies & David J. A. Clines, (Sheffield: Sheffield Academic Press, 1998), 128-135.
Noll, K.L. *The Faces of David.* Sheffield: Sheffield Academic Press, 1997.
O'Brien, Mark A. "The Contribution of Judah's Speech, Genesis 44:18-34, to the Characterization of Joseph", *CBQ* 59/3 (1997): 429-447.
O'Day, Gail. R. "'I have Overcome the World' John 16:33: Narrative Time in John 13-17", *Semeia* 53 (1991): 153-166.
Pamment, Margaret. "Focus in the Fourth Gospel", *ET* 97/3 (1985): 71-75.
Perdue, Leo G. "Is There Anyone Left in the House of Saul...? Ambiguity and the Characterization of David in the Succession Narrative", *JSOT* 30 (1984): 67-84.
Person, Raymond F. *In Conversation with Jonah: Conversation Analysis, Literary Criticism and the Book of Jonah.* Sheffield: Sheffield Academic Press, 1996.
Petersen, Norman R. "Point of View in Mark's Narrative", *Semeia* 12 (1978): 97-121.
Petersen, Norman R. *Literary Criticism for New Testament Critics.* Philadelphia: Fortress, 1978.
Phelan, James. *Reading People, Reading Plots. Character, Progression, and the Interpretation of Narrative.* Chicago: University of Chicago Press, 1989.
Powell, Mark Allan. "The Plots and Subplots of Matthew's Gospel", *NTS* 38/2 (1992): 87-204.
Powell, Mark Allan. "The Religious Leaders in the Gospel of Luke: A Literary-Critical Study", *JBL* 109 (1990): 103-120.
Powell, Mark Allan. *What is Narrative Criticism?* Minneapolis: Fortress, 1990.
Prince, Gerald. "Introduction to the Study of the Narratee", in *Narratology. An Introduction,* eds. Susana Onega & José Angel García Landa, (London: Longman, 1996), 190-202.
Prince, Gerald. "Notes toward a Categorization of Fictional Narratees", *Genre* 4/1 (1971): 100-106.
Prince, Gerald. *A Dictionary of Narratology.* University of Nebraska Press, 1987.
Prince, Gerald. *Narratology. The Form and Functioning of Narrative.* Berlin: Mouton, 1982.
Propp, Vladimir. *Morphology of the Folktale.* Austin: Texas, 1968.
Rapske, Brian M. "Acts, Travel and Shipwreck", in *The Book of Acts in its First Century Setting. Volume 2: Graeco-Roman Setting,* eds. David W. J. Gill, & Conrad Gempf, (Grand Rapids: Eerdmans, 1994), 1-48.
Reinhartz, Adele. "Jesus as Prophet: Predictive Prolepses in the Fourth Gospel", *JSNT* 36 (1989): 3-16.
Resseguie, James L. "John 9: A Literary-Critical Analysis", in *Literary Interpretation of Biblical Narrative. Vol 2,* eds. Kenneth R. R. Gros-Louis & James S. Ackermann, (Nashville: Abingdon, 1982), 295-304.
Resseguie, James L. "Point of View in the Central Section of Luke 5:51-19:44", *JETS* 23 (1982): 41-47.
Rhoads, David & Michie, Donald. *Mark as Story. An Introduction to the Narrative of a Gospel.* Philadelphia: Fortress, 1982.
Rimmon-Kenan, Shlomith. *Narrative Fiction. Contemporary Poetics.* London: Metheuen, 1983.
Rohnen, Ruth. "Paradigm Shifts in Plot Models: An Outline of the History of Narratology", *Poetics Today* 11/4 (1990): 817-842.
Roth, S. John. *The Blind, the Lame and the Poor. Character Types in Luke-Acts.* Sheffield: Sheffield Academic Press, 1997.

Ryan, Mariè-Lauren. *Possible Worlds, Artificial Intelligence and Narrative Theory*. Bloomington: Indiana University Press, 1991.
Schildgren, Brenda Deen. *Crisis and Community. Time in the Gospel of Mark*. Sheffield: Sheffield Academic Press, 1998.
Scholes, Robert & Kellogg, Robert. *The Nature of Narrative*. Oxford: Oxford University Press, 1966.
Segovia, Fernando F. "The Journeys of the Word of God. A Reading of the Plot of the Fourth Gospel", *Semeia* 53 (1991): 23-54.
Sheeley, Steven. "The Narrator in the Gospels: Developing a Model", *PRSt* 16 (1989): 213-223.
Shepherd, William H. *The Narrative Function of the Holy Spirit in Luke-Acts*. Atlanta: Scholars Press, 1994.
Smartley, Willard M. "The Role of Women in Mark's Gospel: A Narrative Analysis", *BTB* 27/1 (1997): 16-22.
Smith, Stephen H. *A Lion with Wings: A Narrative-Critical Approach to Mark's Gospel*. Sheffield: Sheffield Academic Press, 1996.
Smitten, Jeffrey R. & Daghistany, Ann. Eds. *Spatial Form in Narrative*. Ithaca: Cornell, 1981.
Staley, Jeffrey L. "Stumbling in the Dark, Reaching for the Light: Reading Character in John 5 and 9", *Semeia* 53 (1991): 55-80.
Staley, Jeffrey L. *The Print's First Kiss: A Rhetorical Investigation of the Implied Reader in the Fourth Gospel*. Atlanta: Scholars Press, 1988.
Stanton, Robert. *An Introduction to Fiction*. New York: Holt, Rinehart & Winston, 1965.
Stanzel, Franz K. *A Theory of Narrative*. Cambridge: Cambridge University Press, 1984.
Stanzel, Franz K. *Narrative Situations in the Novel*. Bloomington: Indiana University Press, 1955. Translated from the German.
Stanzel, Franz K. *Typische Formen des Romans*. Göttingen: Vandenhoeck & Ruprecht, 1965.
Sternberg, Meir. *The Poetics of Biblical Narrative. Ideological Literature and the Drama of Reading*. Bloomington: Indiana University Press, 1985.
Stibbe, Mark W. G. "A Tomb with a View: John 11:1-44 in Narrative-Critical Perspective", *NTS* 40 (1994): 35-54.
Talbert, Charles H. *Reading Luke: A Literary-Theological Commentary on the Third Gospel*. New York: Crossroad, 1982.
Tannehill, Robert C. *The Narrative Unity of Luke-Acts. A Literary Interpretation. Volume One: The Gospel according to Luke*. Philadelphia: Fortress, 1986.
Thiemann, Ronald F. "The Unnamed Woman at Bethany", *ThTo* 44 (1987): 179-188.
Tilley, Allen. *Plot Snakes and the Dynamics of Narrative Experience*. Gainesville: University Press of Florida, 1992.
Tolmie, D. Francois. "John 21:24-25: A Case of Failed Attestation?", *Skrif en Kerk* 17/2 (1996): 420-426.
Tolmie, D. Francois. "The Characterization of God in the Fourth Gospel", *JSNT* 69 (1998): 57-75.
Tolmie, D. Francois. *Jesus' Farewell to the Disciples. John 13:1-17:26 in Narratological Perspective*. Leiden: E. J. Brill, 1995.
Tovey, Derek. *Narrative Art and Act in the Fourth Gospel*. Sheffield: Sheffield Academic Press, 1997.
Trible, Phyllis. *God and the Rhetoric of Sexuality*. Philadelphia: Fortress, 1978.
Turner, Laurence A. *Announcements of Plot in Genesis*. Sheffield: JSOT, 1990.
Uspensky, Boris. *The Poetics of Composition. The Structure of the Artistic Text and Typology of a Compositional Form*. London: University of California Press, 1973.
Van Aarde, Andries G. "Narrative Point of View: An Ideological Reading of Luke 12:35-48", *Neotest* 22/2 (1988): 235-252.

Van Alphen, Ernst & De Jong, Irene. Eds. *Door het oog van de tekst. Essays voor Mieke Bal over visie*. Muiderberg: Dick Coutinho, 1988.
Van Iersel, Bas. "Locality, Structure and Meaning in Mark", *LingBib* 53 (1983): 45-54.
Van Tilborg, Sjef. "The Gospel of John: communicative processes in a narrative text", *Neotest* 23/1 (1989), 19-31.
Van Tilborg, Sjef. *Al lezend stemmen horen*. Nijmegen: Katholieke Universiteit, 1994.
Van Tilborg, Sjef. *Imaginative Love in John*. Leiden: E J Brill, 1993.
Van Wolde, Ellen J. *A Semiotic Analysis of Genesis 2-3. A Semiotic Theory and Method of Analysis Applied to the Story of the Garden of Eden*. Assen: Van Gorcum, 1989.
Von Rad, Gerhard. *Genesis. A Commentary*. Revised Edition. London: SCM, 1972.
Vorster, Willem S. "Characterization of Peter in the Gospel of Mark", *Neotest* 21 (1987): 57-76.
Vorster, Willem S. "The Reader in the Text: Narrative Material", *Semeia* 48 (1989): 21-39.
Walsh, Jerome T. "Genesis 2:4b-3:24: A Synchronic Approach", *JBL* 96 (1977): 161-177.
Walsh, Jerome T. "The Characterization of Solomon in First Kings 1-5", *CBQ* 57 (1995): 471-493.
Webb, Barry G. *The Book of Judges. An Integrated Reading*. Sheffield: SJOT Press, 1987.
West, Ramona Faye. *Ruth: A Retelling of Genesis 38?* Ann Arbor: University Microfilms International, 1987.
Westermann, Claus. *Genesis 1-11. A Commentary*. Minneapolis: Augsburg, 1974.
White, Hugh C. *Narration and Discourse in the Book of Genesis*. Cambridge: Cambridge University Press, 1991.
Wuellner, Wilhelm. "Narrative Criticism and the Lazarus Story", Paper Read at the Society of New Testament Studies, in Rome (Italy), August 1981.

INDEX OF SUBJECTS

Abigail, 46
Abram, 45
Absalom, 45, 91
Actantial model, 40, 58-59, 123
Actant, 40, 56-58
Agent, 55
Ahimaaz, 46
Anachrony, 89, 93
Analepsis, 88-89, 91-92, 129
Anna, 47
Anterior narration, 15
Background character, 55
Bathsheba, 45
Beloved Disciple, 35, 122, 131, 141-142
Boaz, 49-50
Card, 55
Causality, 67, 74, 81
Characterization, 41-53
    and actions, 44-45
    and environment 44, 47
    and external appearance, 44-45, 47
    and speech 44, 46-47
    direct, 120-121, 138
    indirect, 120-121
    ironical, 44
    paradigm of traits, 41, 50-53, 120-121
Characters, 39-62
    and actions, 39-41
    and events, 67, 74
    classification of, 53-59, 122-123
    complexity of, 56-58
    development of, 56-58

    in text/people in real world, 39-41
    penetration of, 56-58
    purist approach to, 39-40
    realistic approach to, 39-40
    travelling in Hebrew Bible, 107
Chronological setting, 130-131, 133
Complementary relationships, 69
Completing analepsis, 102n.4
Completing prolepsis, 102n.4
Contradictory relationships, 68-69
Contrary relationships, 68-69
Covert narrator, 19-20
David, 45, 91
Deep structure. *See* Events.
Desert (as setting), 110
Direct characterization in Hebrew Bible, 42-43
Direct characterization in New Testament, 43-44
Directing function (of narrator), 21-22
Disciples, 58, 121
Discipleship, 126-127, 135, 138, 140-141
Duration. *See* Time.
Durative event, 65, 125
Eglon, 46
Ehud, 46
Ellipsis, 94-95, 97
Embedded analepsis, 87, 93, 129
Embedded narrative
    explicative function, 17
    thematic function, 17-18
Embedded prolepsis, 87, 93, 129

INDEX OF SUBJECTS

Esau, 46
Evaluative perspective, 116
Events, 63-84
    classification of, 64, 123-124
    deep structure of, 67-69, 126-129, 131
    definition of, 63
    internal relationship between, 67, 75
    paraphrasing of, 64
    principles of combination of, 66-67
    relationship between, 64
    surface structure of, 64-67, 123-124, 131
External analepsis, 102n.4
External event, 65
External prolepsis, 102n.4
Extradiegetic narratee, 16, 25-26
Extradiegetic narrator, 16-17, 25-26, 118
Ficelle, 55, 122
Flat character, 54-55, 57, 122
Focalization, 29-37, 119-120
    definition of, 30-31, 38n.11
    external 32-33, 36-37, 119, 135
    internal 32-33, 36-37, 134, 142-143
    locus of, 32-33, 35, 119
Focalized object, 32-33, 119
    external focalization of, 32-33, 34-35
    internal focalization of, 32-33, 35-36
Form criticism, 2
Formalism, 5, 40
Frequency. *See* Time.
Full-fledged character, 55
Function of attestation, 23, 27n.9
Galilee (as setting), 110
Generative trajectory, 68
Gentile territory (as setting), 113
Glorification (in Gospel according to John), 132-133
Goliath, 46
Helper (actant), 57-59
Herod, 46, 92,
Heterodiegetic analepsis, 102n.4
Heterodiegetic narratee, 25-26
Heterodiegetic narrator, 18-19, 25-26, 118
Hinneh
    use of in Hebrew Bible, 34
Homer, 3
Homodiegetic narratee, 18
Homodiegetic narrator, 18
Homodiegetic prolepsis, 102n.4
Hypodiegetic narratee, 16-18

Hypodiegetic narrator, 16
Ideological function, 22-23, 118-119
Ideological perspective, 7, 116, 132-135, 142-143
Implied author, 6-7, 11n.22, 11n.28, 25, 115-142
Implied reader, 7-9, 11n.24; 11n.28, 115-142
Indirect characterization in Hebrew Bible, 45-46
Indirect characterization in New Testament, 46-48
Internal event, 65
Intradiegetic narratee, 16-18, 25
Intradiegetic narrator, 16-17, 25
Isotopy, 68, 75, 81
Iterative frequency, 100
Jael, 97
Jairus, 47
Jephthah, 91
Jerusalem (as setting), 110-111
Jesus, 58, 120-121, 137-138, 141
John the Baptist, 47, 92
Jordan (as setting), 112
Joseph, 45
Judas Iscariot, 50-53, 58, 122, 131, 134-135
Kadesh-barnea, 108
Kernels, 65
Lake (as setting), 110
Linearity, 8-9
Macrosequence (of events), 66
Meal scenes, 111
Microsequence (of events), 66, 123-124
Moses, 19,
Mountains (as setting), 108-110
Narratee, 13-27, 117-119
    definition of, 13-14
    degree of perceptibility of, 19-20, 25-26
    extent of participation of, 18-19
    reliability of, 20-21
    temporal relations, 15-16
Narrative aside, 118
Narrative criticism, 1, 4, 10n.1
Narrative criticism,
    history of, 2-5
Narrative critics, 5
Narrative pause, 93-94, 138
Narratological framework, 5-7
Narratologists, 5
Narratology, 1, 10n.1

INDEX OF SUBJECTS

Narrator, 11n.22, 13-27, 117-119
   and focalization, 31-32
   definition of, 13-14
   degree of perceptibility of, 19-20, 25-26, 118
   extent of participation, 18-19
   functions of, 21-23
   in Jonah, 24-25
   in the Gospel of Luke: 25
   narrative levels, 16-18
   reliability of, 20-21, 25-26, 118
   speech of, 25
   temporal relations, 15-16
New Criticism, 5
Object (actant), 57-59
Og, 108
Opponent (actant), 57-59
Order. *See* Time.
Overt narrator, 19-20
Paraclete, 58
Paradigm of traits. *See* Characterization. Movement
   Pattern of in Mark, 112-113
Paul, 36-37, 77-82
Peter, 35-36, 58, 122, 131, 137, 142
Phenomenology of Reading, 5
Plot, 4, 63, 125
   of Acts 27:1-44, 77-82
   of Genesis 2:4b-3:25, 72-75
   of Gospel according to John, 132
Point of view, 22, 29-30, 38n.7, 38n.14
Private settings, 112
Process of deterioration, 73, 80
Process of improvement, 73
Prolepsis, 87-89, 91
Protagonist, 55, 122
Public settings, 112
Punctual event, 65, 125
Rachel, 45
Reader-Response Criticism, 5
Real author, 6, 11n.22
Real reader, 6
Receiver (actant), 57-59
Redaction criticism, 2
Reliability of narrators in Hebrew Bible, 21
Reliability of narrators in New Testament, 21
Repeating prolepsis, 102n.4
Repetitive frequency, 100
Round character, 54-55, 57, 123

Russian Formalism, 5
Ruth, 48-50
Satellites, 65-66
Saul, 45
Scenic representation, 94-95, 129, 133, 135, 142
Sea (as setting), 112
Semiotic square, 67-69, 75, 81-82, 126
Sender (actant), 57-59
Setting, 105-114, 130, 136, 143
   in Biblical narratives, 107-108
   in Deuteronomy 107-108
   significance of, 106
Sihon, 108
Simultaneous narration, 15
Singulative frequency, 100
Sisera, 95-96
Slowdown, 94-95
Social settings, 111-112
Source criticism, 2
Space and events, 67, 74-75, 81
Spatial setting, 130-131, 134
Speed of a narrative, 93, 95, 97-98
Spheres of action, 40
Story level, 88
Story-time, 4, 93-94, 95-96
Structuralism, 5, 40, 56
Subject (actant), 57-59
Summary, 94-95, 97, 98-99
Suspense, 140-141
Synagogue (as setting), 110
Tamar, 45
Temple (as setting), 111
Temporal relations. *See* Time.
Temporality, 8-9, 132
Testimonial function, 23
Text-time, 93-99
Textual strategy, 130
Thomas, 58
Time, 87-103
   and events, 67, 74, 81
   duration, 93-99, 129
   duration in John 13:1-17:26, 97-99
   duration in Judges 4, 95-97
   frequency, 99-101, 129
   frequency in Biblical narratives, 100-101
   order, 87-93, 129
   order in 2 Samuel 17:24-18:33, 91
   order in Judges 10:6-12:7, 90-91

order in Mark 6:7-30, 92
Trait, 41, 50-53, 131, 137
Type, 55
Ulterior narration 15, 25

Unreliable narratee, 21
Unreliable narrator, 20
World, 58

INDEX OF AUTHORS

Alter, Robert, 9, 62n.19
Amit, Yairah, 26, 27n.6
Auerbach, Erich, 2-3, 10nn.4-5
Bal, Mieke, 5, 11n.17, 26, 27n.1, 37, 38n.11, 59, 82, 101, 102n.13
Barat, Karen A., 83
Bar-Efrat, Shimon, 3, 9, 10n.3, 10n.10, 26, 27n.3, 38n.7, 46, 60, 61n.12, 83, 85n.21, 85n.28, 101, 102nn.8-9, 113, 114n.3,
Barthes, Roland, 83
Bartholomew, Gilbert, 37
Beardslee, William A., 9
Beekman, K. D., 62n.24
Berendsen, Marjet, 37
Berlin, Adele, 3, 9, 10n.9, 26, 34, 37, 38n.14, 55, 60, 62n.26
Black, C. Clifton III, 60
Boers, Hendrikus, 83
Boomershine, Thomas, 37
Booth, Wayne C., 6-7, 11n.21, 29, 38n.5
Boulton, Marjorie, 38n.6
Brenner, Athalya, 60
Brink, André P., 84n.10
Brooks, Cleanth, 29-30, 38n.2, 38n.8
Brooks, Peter, 82, 84n.2
Brown, Raymond E., 62n.22
Campbell, Edward J., 61n.14, 61n.20
Carter, Warren, 83
Caserio, Robert L., 82
Caspi, Michael Maswari, 26
Chatman, Seymour, 5, 7, 11n.18, 11n.20, 11n.22, 26, 27n.5, 41-42, 59, 61n.7, 64-66, 73, 82, 84n.5, 84nn.8-9, 85n.24, 101, 113
Cixous, Helene, 59
Claassens, L. M. J., 101
Clines, David, J. A., 9
Cohan, Steven, 10n.1, 26, 37, 59, 62n.30, 63, 82, 84n.1, 84n.3, 84n.15, 101
Cohn, Robert L., 108, 113, 114n.5
Cooper, Alan, 83
Courtés, J., 84n.12
Craig, Kenneth M., 24, 27n.10
Creech, R. Robert, 26
Crittenden, Charles, 59
Culley, Robert C., 83, 84n.10
Culpepper, R. Alan, 26, 60, 83, 97, 99, 101, 103n.17, 103n.19
Daghistany, Ann, 113
Danove, Paul, 60
Darr, John A., 60
Dawsey, James M., 25-26, 27n.12
Day, Linda, 60
De Jong, Irene, 38n.11
Deist, Ferdinand E., 26, 54-55, 62n.25
Dembinski, Jos, 38n.11
Eco, Umberto, 9, 11n.25
Edminston, William F., 37
Edwards, O. C., 11n.14
Edwards, Richard A., 11n.14
Eslinger, Lyle, 26
Ewen, Joseph, 56, 58, 62n.28
Ferraro, Fernando, 40, 61n.5
Fewell, Danna Nolan, 21, 26, 27n.7, 43, 60,

61n.9, 61n.16, 83
Fields, Weston F., 113
Fokkelman, Jan P., 102n.10
Fontijn, J., 62n.24
Forster, E. M., 54-55, 57, 59, 62n.23
Fowler, Robert M., 11n.23, 26, 37, 38n.7
Fowler, Roger, 37
Friedman, Norman, 29, 38n.4
Frye, Northrop, 3, 9, 10nn.6-7
Funk, Robert W., 9, 26, 102
Garvey, James, 59
Genette, Gérard, 5, 10n.1, 11n.15, 26, 27n.8, 31, 34, 37, 38nn.11-12, 86, 93, 101, 102nn.1-4, 102nn.12-13, 103n.18, 103n.20
Gowler, David B., 60
Green, Barbara, 60, 83
Greimas, A. J., 40, 56-59, 62n.29, 67-69, 84n.12
Gunkel, Herman, 2, 10n.2
Gunn, David M., 9, 21, 26-27, 27n.7, 43, 60, 61n.9, 61n.16, 83
Haenchen, Ernst, 85n.31
Hallberg, Calinda Ellen, 83
Harvey, W. J., 55-56, 58-59, 62n.27
Hauser, Alan John, 9, 85n.27
Hawk, L. Daniel, 83
Hedrick, Charles W., 27
Herman, David, 37
Hochman, Baruch, 59
Holleran, J. Warren, 38n7, 102, 113
Howell, David B., 102
Hubbard, Robert L., 61n.15, 62n.18
Humphreys, W. Lee, 83
Iser, Wolfgang, 9, 11n.25
Jasper, Alison, 37
Jeansonne, Sharon Pace, 60
Jobling, David, 68, 83, 84n.14, 85nn.22-23, 85n.30
Kanzog, Klaus, 38n.6
Kelber, Werner H., 11n.14, 92, 102n.11
Kellogg, Robert, 38n.6
Kenney, William, 59, 113
Kermode, Frank, 9
Kingsbury, Jack Dean, 11n.14, 60, 83, 114n.6
Kisling, Paul J., 60
Klauck, Hans-Josef, 60
Knott, William C., 38n.6
Kunin, Seth D., 83

Kurz, William S., 11n.24, 27, 37, 38n.7, 38n.16, 83
Lambe, Anthony J., 83
Lanning, George, 38n.6, 113
Lategan, Bernard C., 11n.23
Licht, Jacob, 38n.7, 102, 102nn.14-15
Longman, Tremper, 10
Lubbock, Percy, 29, 38n.1
Macauley, Robie, 38n.6, 113
Maccoby, Hyam, 62n.21
Malbon, Elizabeth Struthers, 60, 113
Malina, Bruce J., 114n.2
Martin, Wallace, 37, 38n.11, 59, 83, 101
Matera Frank J., 83
McConville, J. G., 114n.4
McKnight, Edgar, 10
Menn, Esther Marie, 37
Michie, Donald, 4, 11n.13, 38n.7, 84, 113, 114n.7
Millar, J. G., 114n.4
Moloney, Francis J., 11n.28
Moore, Stephen D., 10, 10n.11, 27, 61n.3
Mudrick, Marvin, 59, 61n.2
Nelles, William, 37
Nicol, George G., 83
Noegel, Scott B., 113
Noll, K. L., 60
O'Brien, Mark A., 60
O'Day, Gail R., 102
Pamment, Margaret, 37
Perdue, Leo G., 60
Person, Raymond F., 60, 84
Petersen, Norman R., 4, 10, 11n.12, 38n.7
Phelan, James, 60
Powell, Mark Allan, 10, 11n.19, 38n.7, 61, 84, 102, 113
Prince, Gerald, 26, 27nn.1-2, 37, 60, 83, 101, 113, 114n.1
Propp, Vladimir, 40, 61n.4
Rapske, Brian M., 85nn.32-33
Reinhartz, Adele, 102
Resseguie, James L., 38n.7, 84
Rhoads, David, 4, 11n.13, 38n.7, 84, 113, 114n.7
Rimmon-Kenan, Shlomith, 5, 11n.16, 26, 27n.4, 37, 38n.11, 38n.13, 40, 61n.1, 61n.6, 61n.8, 61n.10, 62n.28, 67, 84nn.3-4, 84nn.10-11, 101, 102n.3, 102n.14, 103n.18, 103n.21, 113
Rohnen, Ruth, 83

Rohrbaugh, Richard L., 114n.2
Roth, S. John, 61
Ryan, Mariè-Lauren, 83
Schildgren, Brenda Deen, 102
Scholes, Robert, 38n.6
Segovia, Fernando F., 84
Sheeley, Steven, 27
Shepherd, William H., 61
Shires, Linda M., 10n.1, 26, 37, 59, 62n.30, 63, 82, 84n.1, 84n.3, 84n.15, 101
Smartley, Williard M., 61
Smith, Stephen H., 37, 84, 102
Smitten, Jeffrey R., 113
Staley, Jeffrey L., 8-10, 11n.22, 11nn.27-28, 27, 61
Stanton, Robert, 38n.6
Stanzel, Franz K., 26, 29-30, 38n.3, 38n.9
Sternberg, Meir, 3, 10, 10n.8, 21, 27, 27n.3, 27n.6, 45, 61, 61n.11, 85n.20
Stibbe, Mark W. G., 37
Talbert, Charles H., 11n.14
Tannehill, Robert C., 27n.11
Thiemann, Ronald F., 61
Tilley, Allen, 83
Tolmie, D. Francois, 27, 27n.9, 61, 61n.13, 62n.31, 84n.7, 102n.5, 102n.16, 144n.1
Tovey, Derek, 38
Trible, Phyllis, 62n.16
Turner, Laurence A., 84
Uspensky, Boris, 30, 38n.10
Van Aarde, Andries G., 38n.7
Van Alphen, Ernst, 38n.11
Van Iersel, Bas, 113
Van Tilborg, Sjef, 10, 11n.22
Van Wolde, Ellen J., 84, 84n.13, 84nn.16-17, 85n.30
Von Rad, Gerhard, 85nn.18-19, 85n.25
Vorster, Willem S., 8, 11n.22, 11n.26, 61
Walsh, Jerome T., 61, 85n.29
Warren, Robert Penn, 29-30, 38n.2, 38n.8
Webb, Barry G., 102nn.6-7
West, Ramona Faye, 62n.17
Westermann, Claus, 85n.26
White, Hugh, 27
Wuellner, Wilhelm, 84n.6

INDEX OF SCRIPTURE REFERENCES

OLD TESTAMENT

Genesis
2:4b-3:25	69-77
4:1-16	45
6:9	42
12:1-4	45
13:13	42
22	3
27:11	46
29:17	45
32:32	14
38:15	35
39:1-23	45

Deuteronomy
1:1-5	107-108
11:11	109

Joshua
10-12	21

Judges
1	21
3:15	46
3:17	46
4	95-97
4:22	34
6:2	109
9:7	109
10:6-12:7	90-91

Ruth
1-4	48-50

2:1	62n.20
3:11	62n.20

1 Samuel
1:3	100
1:9-18	33-34
17	21
17:4	46
25:24-31	46

2 Samuel
11:2	45
11:27-12:5	17
13:1	45
13:3	43
13:18	14
16:7	43
17:24-18:33	91
18:29	46
21:19	21

1 Kings
11:41	23
14:19	23
14:29	23

2 Kings
13:19	35
23:25	22-23

2 Chronicles
13:4-12	109
27:7	23

28:26	23	27:3-10	51-52
Nehemiah		**Mark**	
1:1	19	1:4	47
7:2	42	3:14-19	51
		5:2	47
Esther		5:42	47
7:6	43	6:51-52	35
		6:7-30	92
Job		8:29	43
1:1	42	12:1-12	17
15:7	109	12:41-44	46
		14:10-11	51
Psalms		14:18-21	51
65:6	109	14:43-45	51
97:5	109	15:39	43
121:1	109		
		Luke	
Daniel		1:1-4	15, 25
1:8	45	1:6	43
6:10	101	1:80	110
7:1	106	2:25	43
		2:25-35	111
Hosea		2:36-40	111
4:13	109	2:37	47
		2:41	101
Obadiah		2:42	47
3	109	4:1	110
		4:14-15	110
Jonah		4:16-30	110
1-4	24-25	4:44	110
		5:4-7	110
NEW TESTAMENT		6:12	110
Matthew		6:13-16	52
2:1-12	46	6:6-11	110
2:3	35	8:22-25	110
3:4	47	9:28	110
5-7	20	9:28-36	111
10:1-4	51	9:29-36	110
10:23	93	9:51-19:46	111
13:41	93	9:53	111
16:18	93	13:10-17	110
16:21	93	13:22	111
16:27	93	13:33	111
17:22	93	17:11	111
20:17	93	17:25	111
24-25	93	18:18-30	46
26:14-16	51-52	18:31-33	111
26:20-25	51	19:28	111
26:47-50	51	21:1-4	111

21:21	110	18:1-1	53
22:21-23	52	18:12-27	35-36
22:3-6	52	20:30-31	22, 23
22:39	110	21:24	23
24:47	111	21:24-25	27n.9
27:47-48	52		

John

Acts

2:11	22	1:8	111
3:2	44	1:15-20	52
4:12	44	2:44-47	101
4:54	22	4:19-20	47
6:70-71	53	4:22	47
8:48	44	6:5	43
12:1-8	53	9:1-18	36-37
13:1-30	53, 116-144	9:36	43
13:1-17:26	57-58; 97-99	22:6-16	36-37
13:2	35, 53	26:12-18	38n.15
13:4	47	27:1-44	77-82
13:30	53		
13:31-17:26	20	**2 Thessalonians**	
17:12	53	2:3	53

www.ingramcontent.com/pod-product-compliance
Lightning Source LLC
Chambersburg PA
CBHW050846160426
43192CB00011B/2165